How to Draw Everything for Kids

101 Cute Drawings of Cute Stuff, Animals, Food, Desserts, Clothes, Garden, and More!

Created by
Ari Penrose

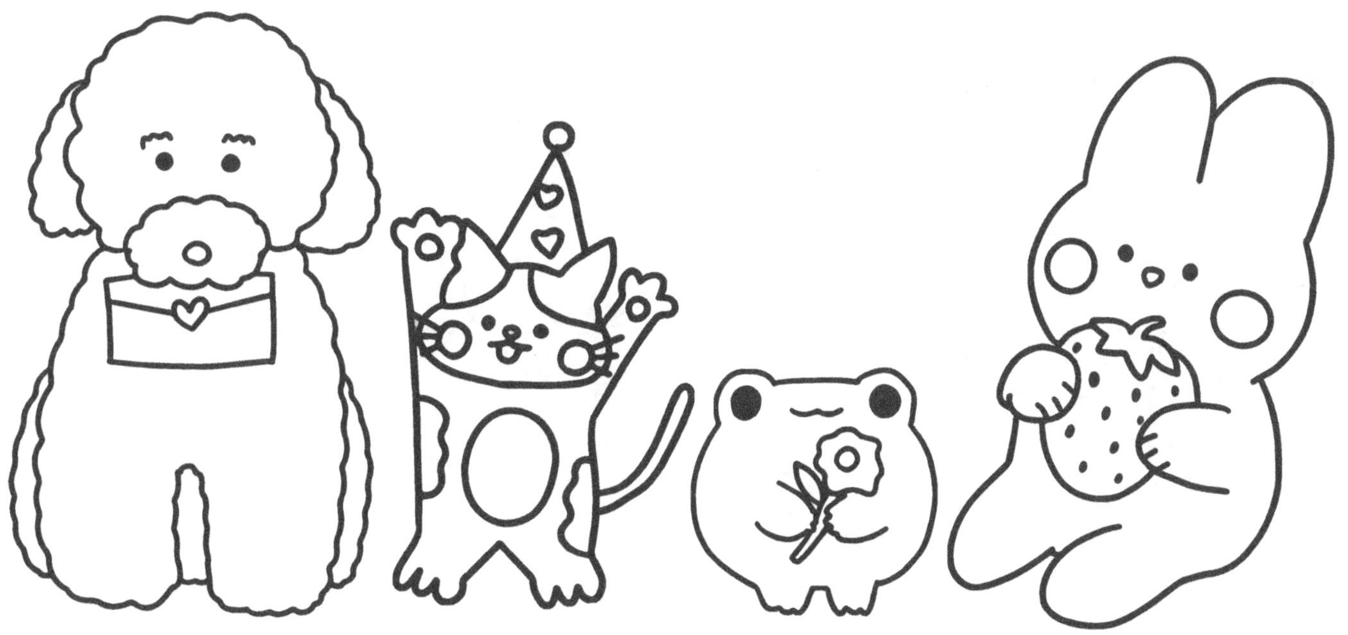

Title: How to Draw Everything for Kids: 101 Cute Drawings of Cute Stuff, Animals, Food, Desserts, Clothes, Garden, and More!

Author:Ari Penrose

Illustrator : Ari Penrose

Art Director : Rocker Martin

Cover Design: Rocker Martin

Edition: 1

Series : Cute Creations Drawing

Published by Rocker Martin

House No.98. Village
No. 5 Nongpho Sub-district Nong Ya Sai District Suphan Buri
Rockermartinofficial@gmail.com

Print at Danex Intercorporation Co., Ltd.,
99/164 M.2 Chaengwatthana Road, Thung Song Hong
Leksi District, Bangkok 10210
Tel. 02-575-1791-3

Printed in Thailand

ISBN : 978-616-616-888-4

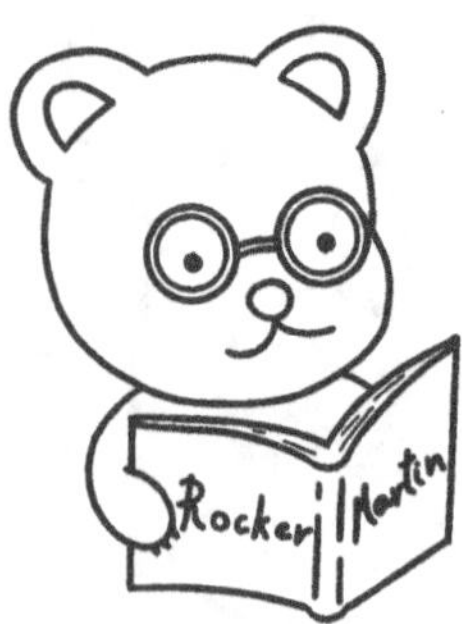

Contents

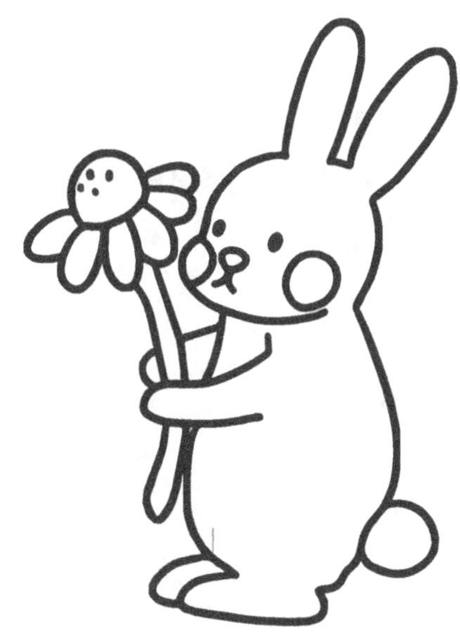

How to Use This Book

- - - - - - - - - - - -

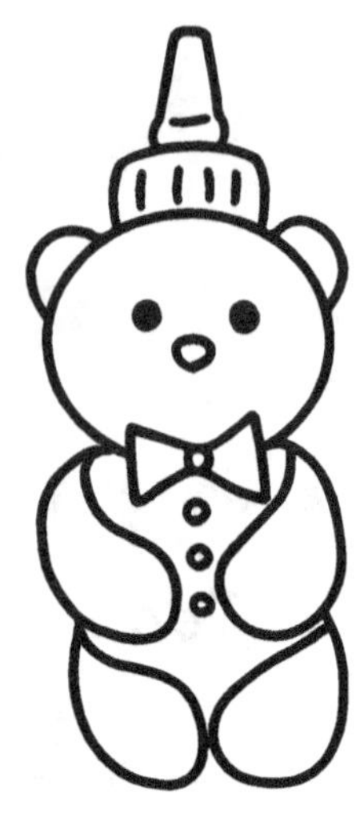

How to Draw the Cutest Things shows you
how to draw more than 101 adorable characters,
including animals, food, household items, and more.
Each character has step-by-step instructions
to help you create your own cute drawing.

Tools

- - -

Creating adorable images does not require expensive equipment.
Use pen and paper or a computer application to draw.
Your decision will come to pass.

BLACK PENS & PENCIL

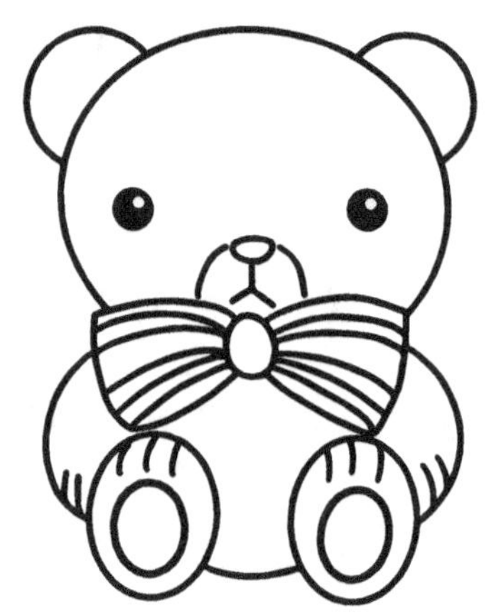

I like using different pens with various tip sizes:

- Thin tips for details, patterns, and shadows.
- Medium tips for outlining characters.
- Thick tips for filling large areas.

WHITE PENS

These are great for adding highlights
and making your drawings pop!

ERASER

Mistakes happen, and that's okay! Always keep
a good eraser nearby.

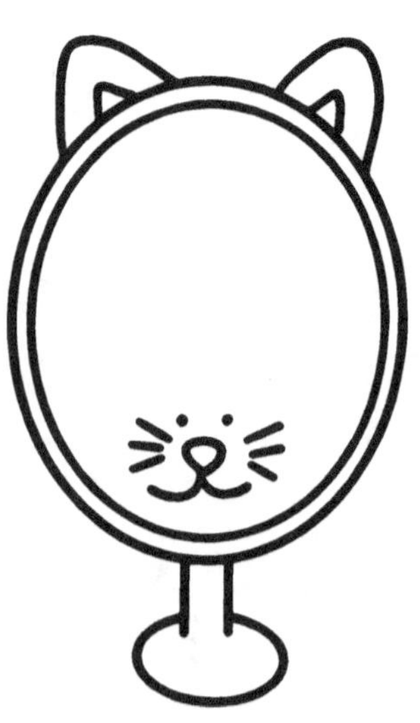

PAPER

Use whatever paper you have in hand!
Whether it is a sketchbook or regular
printer paper, anything works.

TiPs & Tricks

1. Get your pencil and eraser ready. Depending on your preferred style, markers or pense can also be used.

2. Start with light strokes. When drawing, make the first stroke lighter to fix mistakes or erase extra lines.

3. Cut out sharp shapes. When drawing square, rectangular, or pointy shapes, rounding the corners and edges makes your characters appear thinner.

4. Time to color Once you have finished drawing, you can start coloring in any way you like.

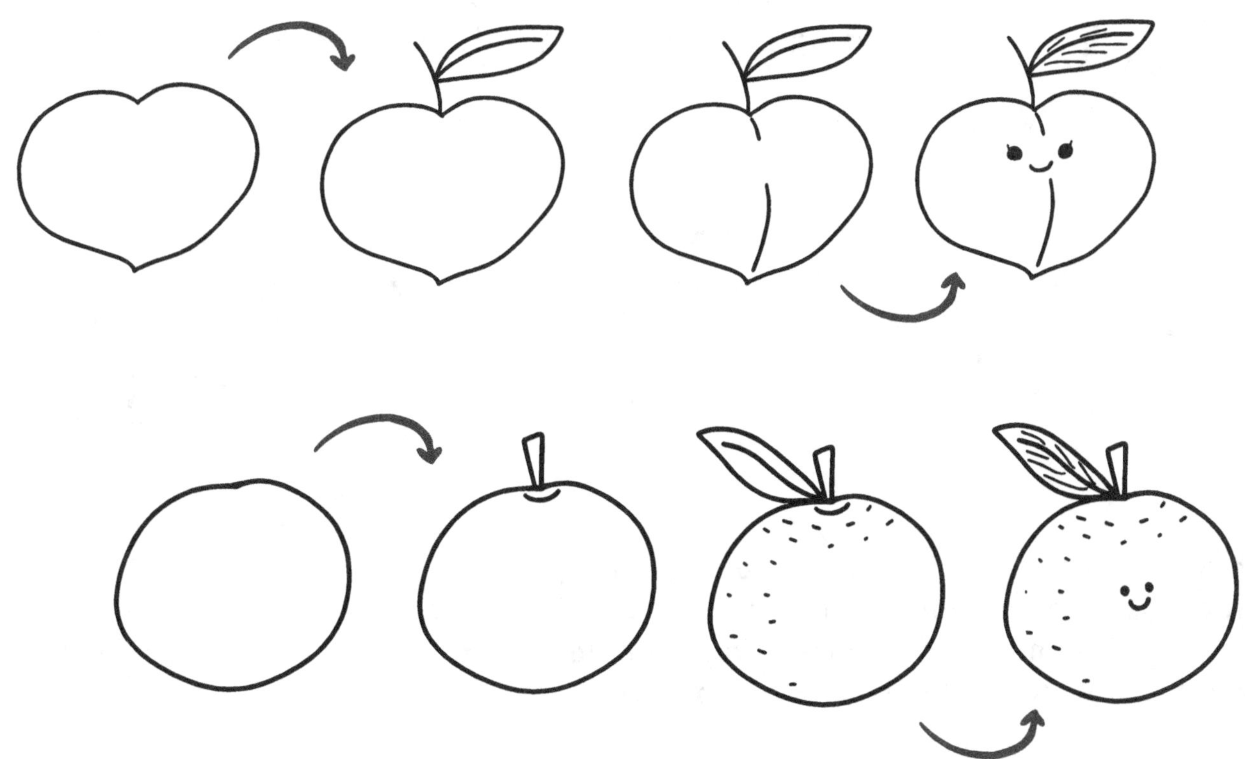

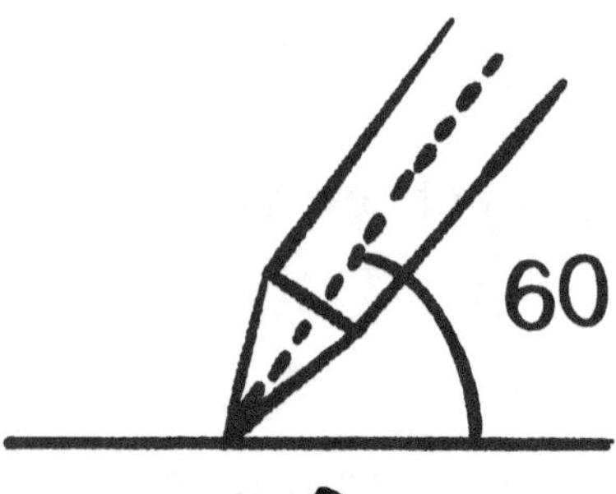

Hold the pen at a 60° angle.
This angle will help you better control your lines.

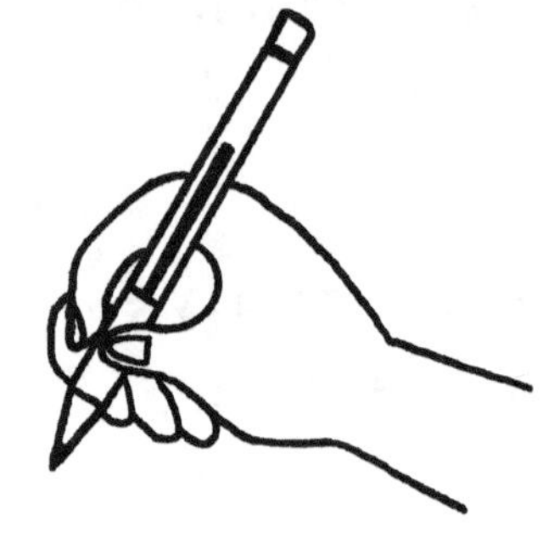

The correct way to hold a pen.
Ensure that the grip is comfortable and not too tight.

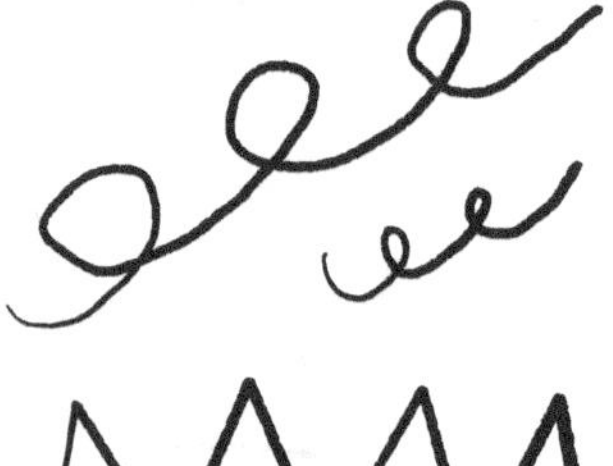

Practice with simple lines.
Get used to using your pen
Or a pencil by drawing curly and zigzag lines.
Doing this every day will improve your control.

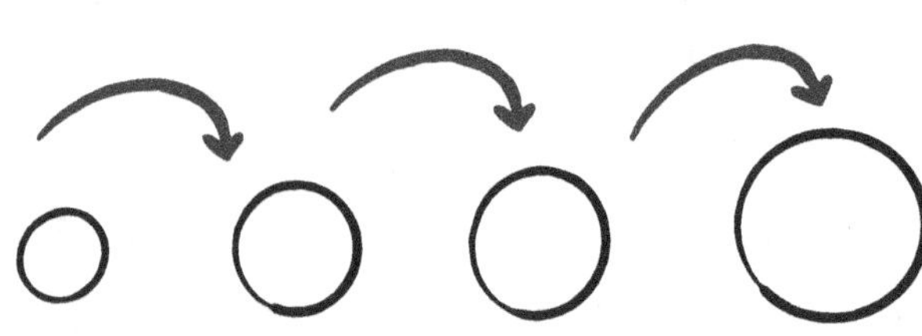

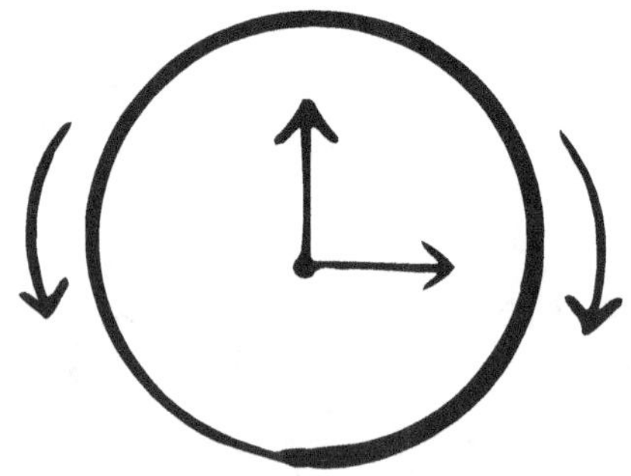

Begin using circles. Start by making small,
Clockwise circles and gradually increase their size.
(For right-handers, this direction is easier.) Left-handers tend to rotate
counterclockwise. Angle the pen at 60°.

Let's Start

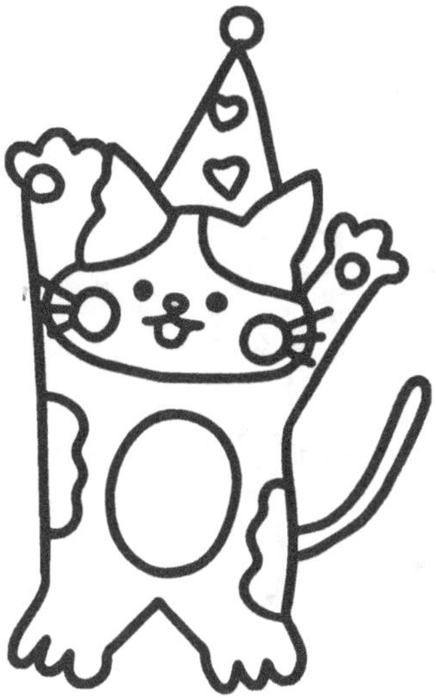

My purpose is to provide you with various cute illustrations while illustrating how to draw them.

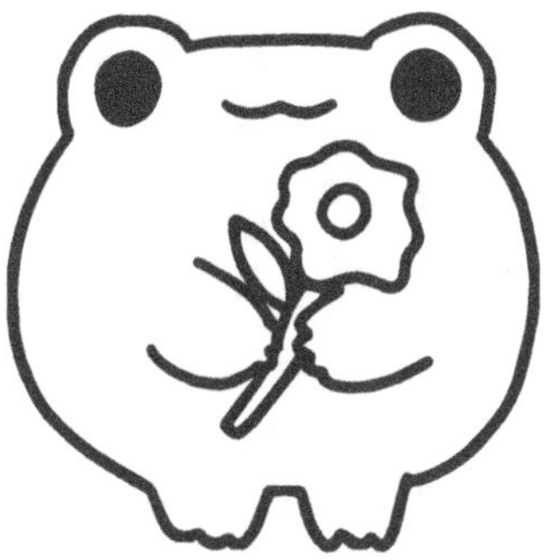

Rabbit and Strawberry

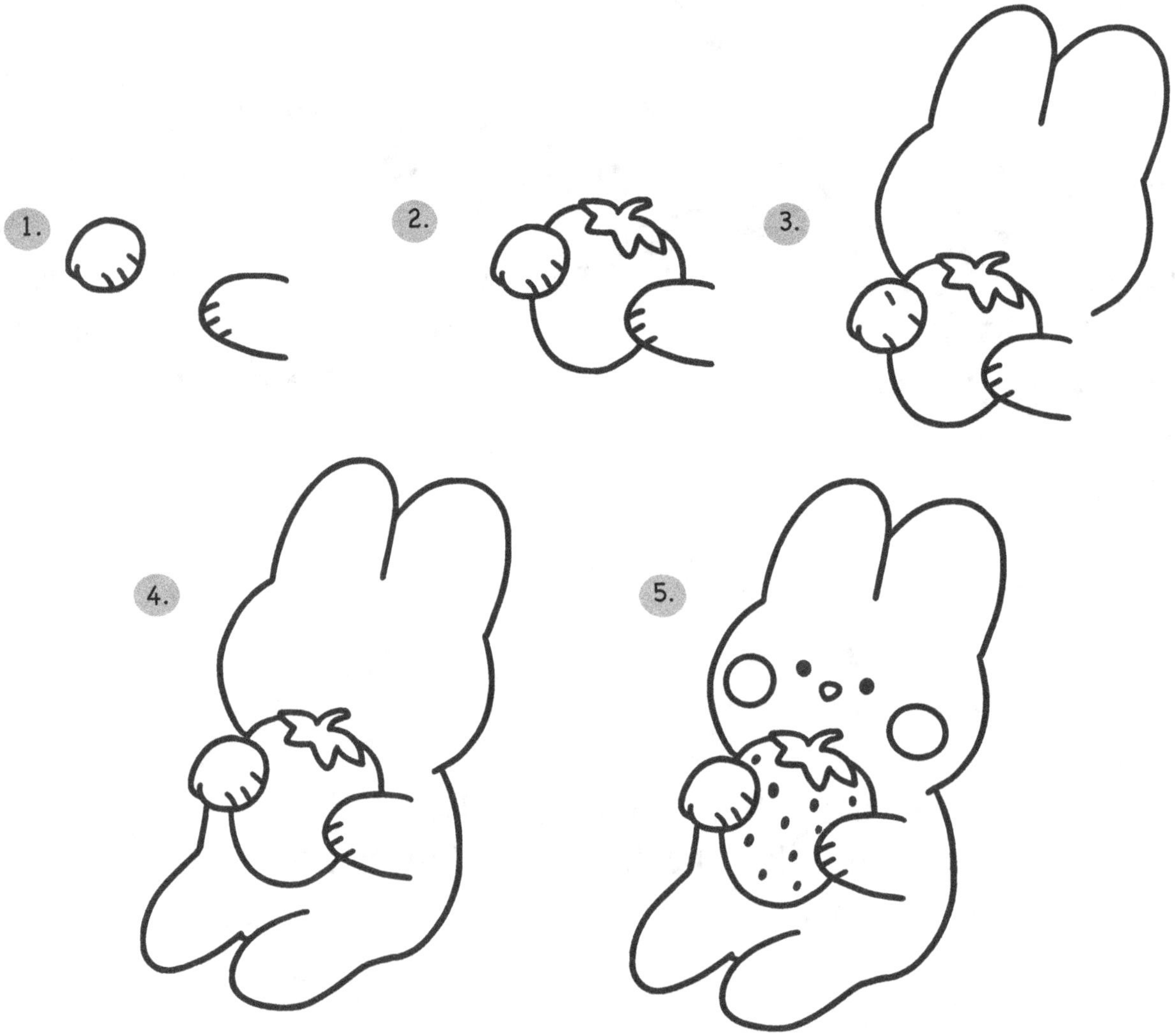

Practice for drawing here.

Dog carries letter

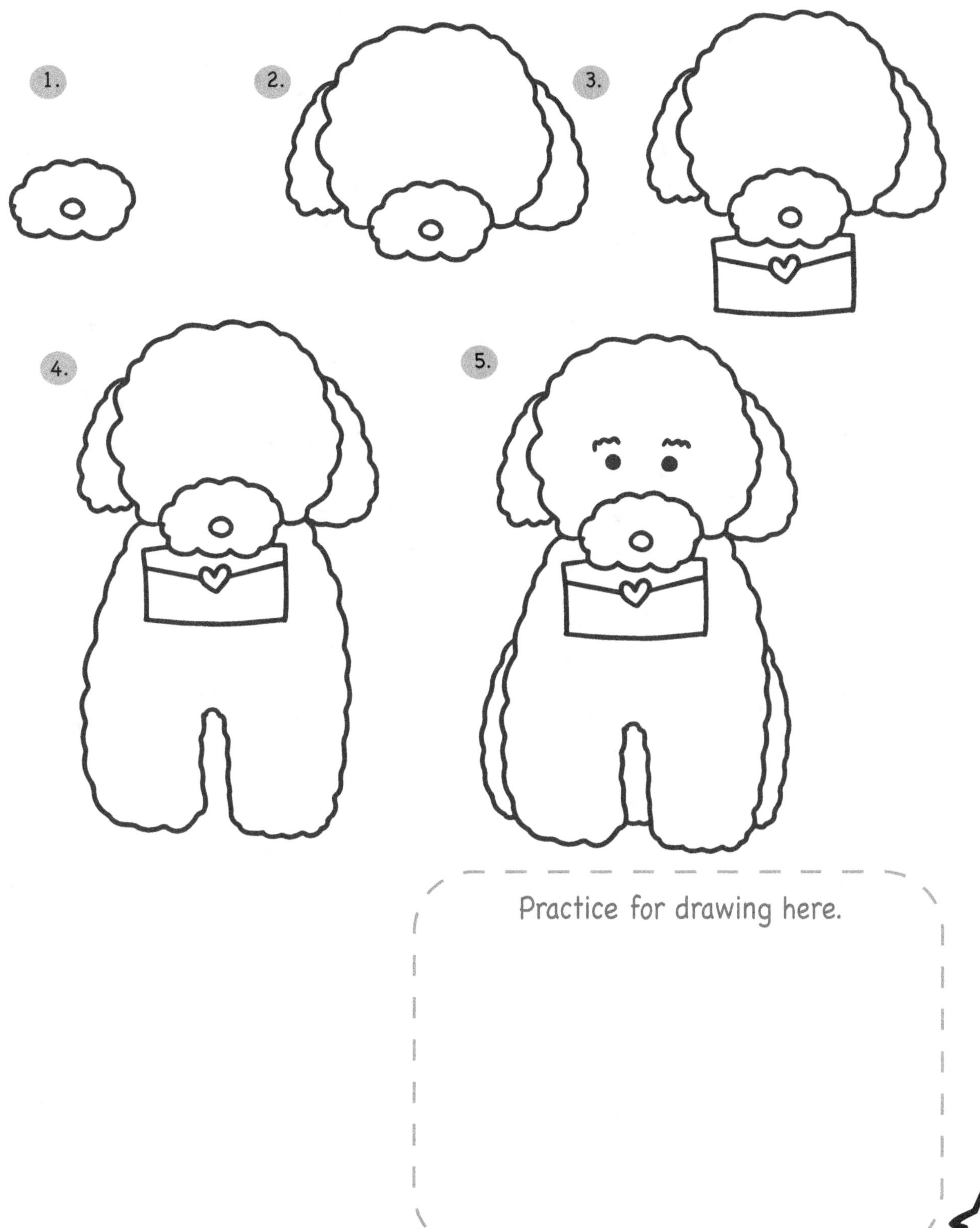

Capybara

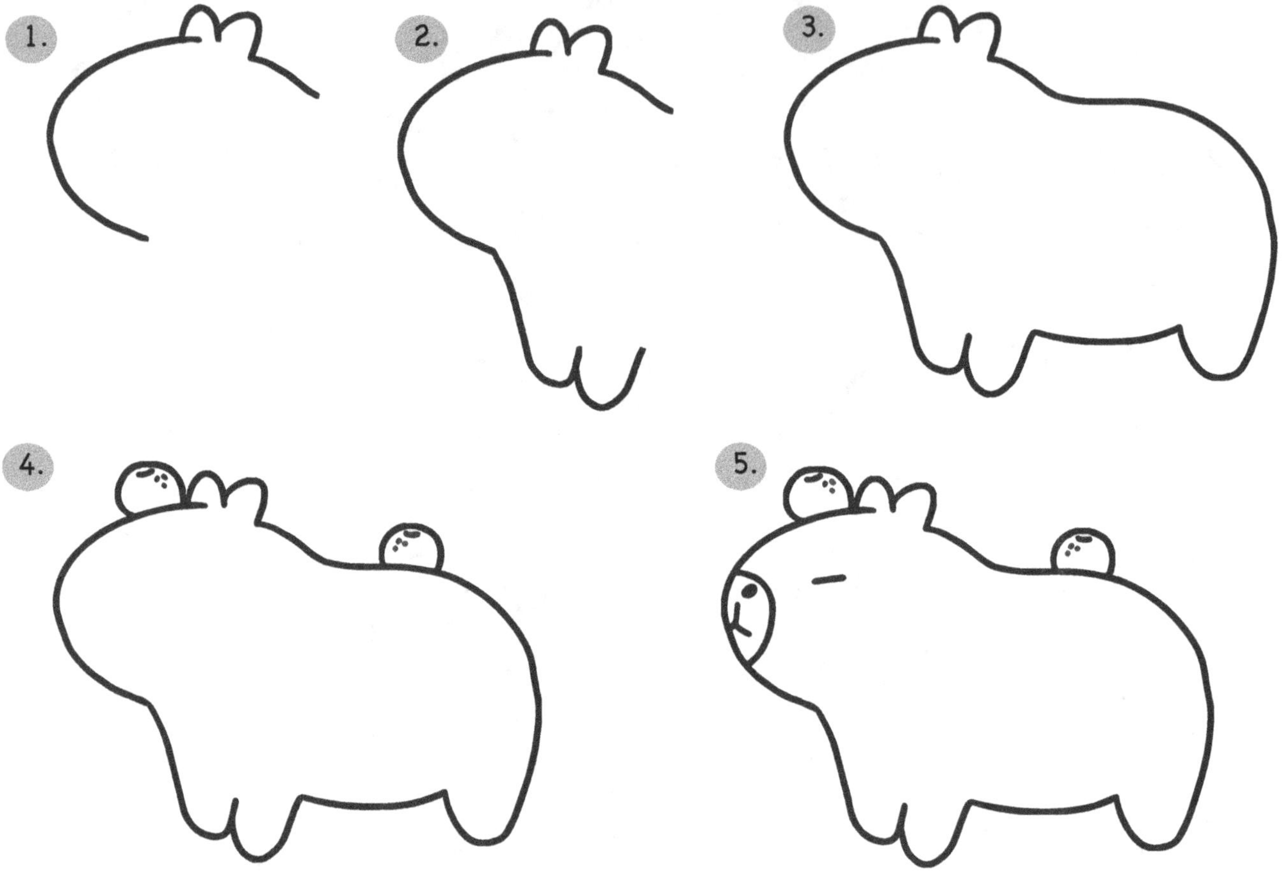

1.
2.
3.
4.
5.

Practice for drawing here.

Rabbit and A Daisy

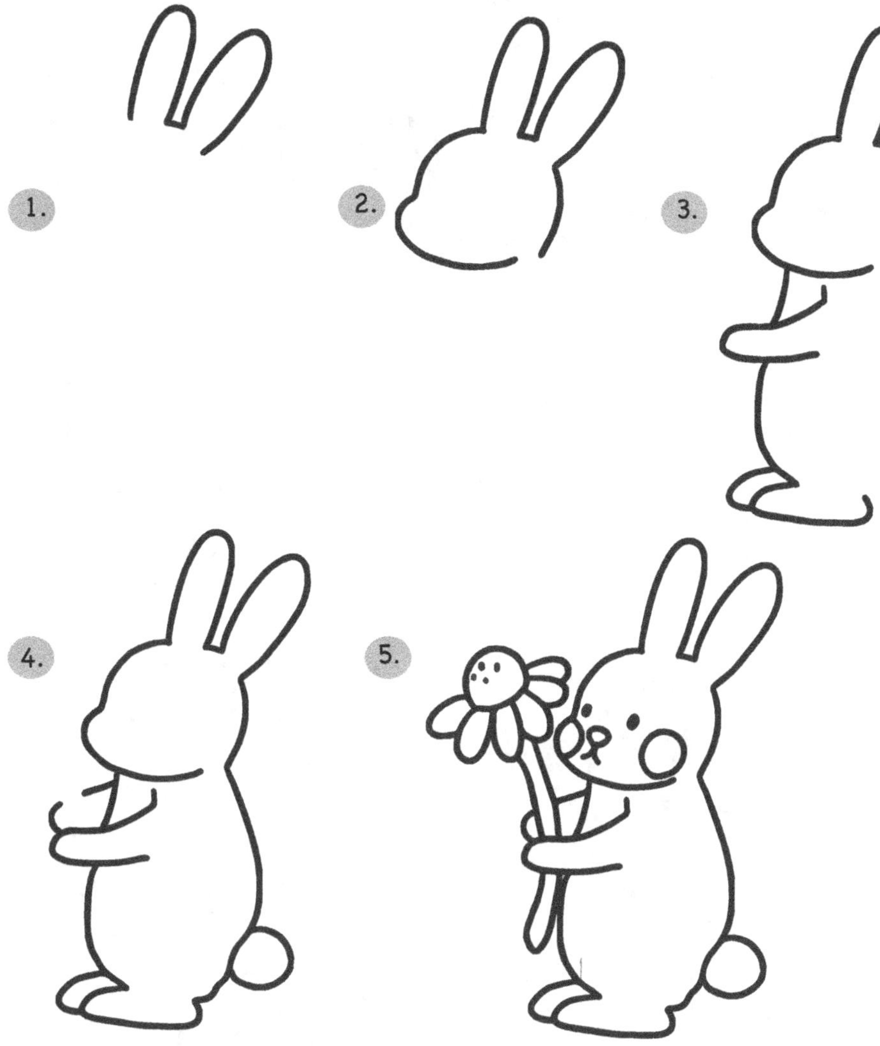

1.

2.

3.

4.

5.

Practice for drawing here.

Party Cat

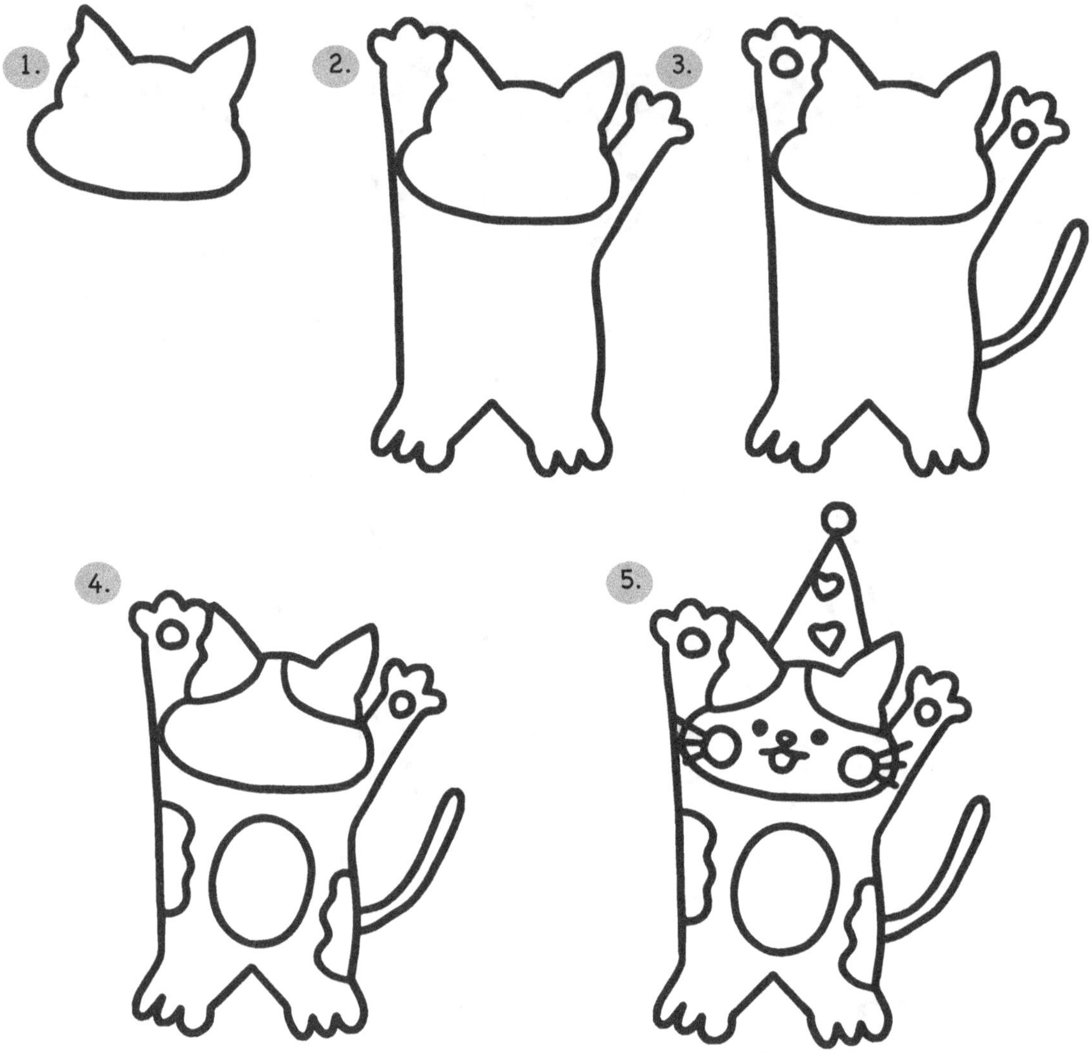

Practice for drawing here.

Frog And A Flower

1.

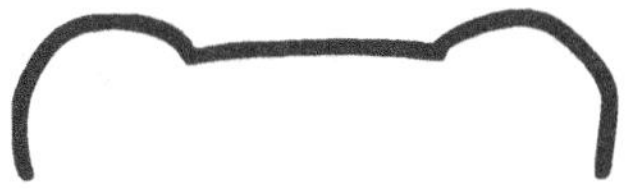

2.

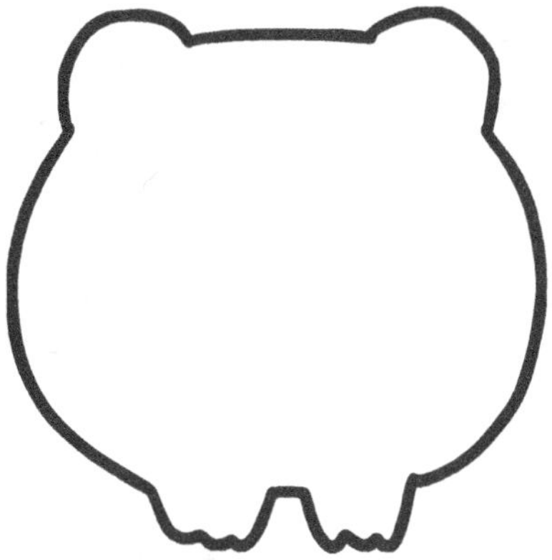

3.

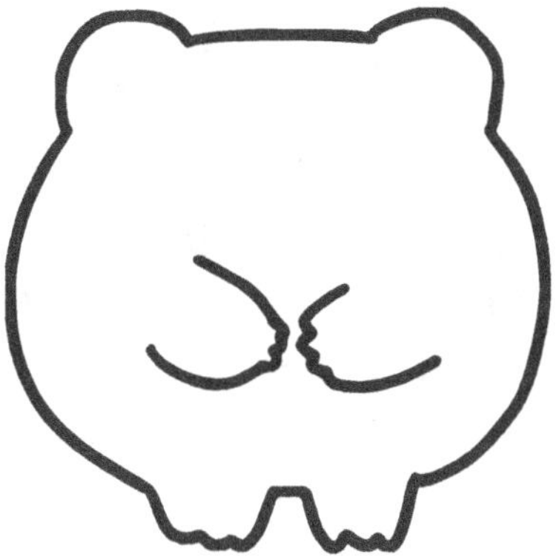

4.

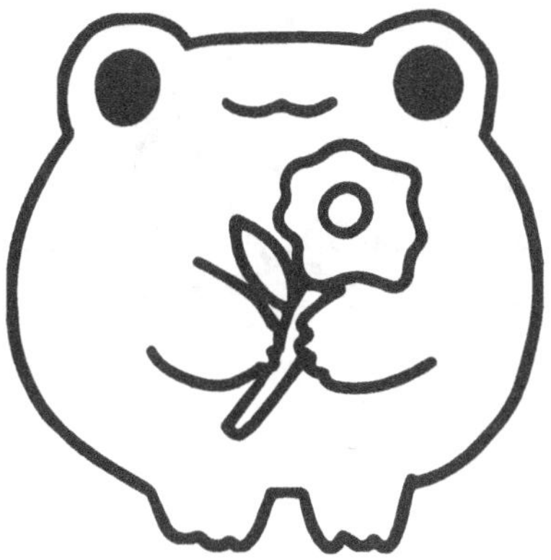

Practice for drawing here.

Bee

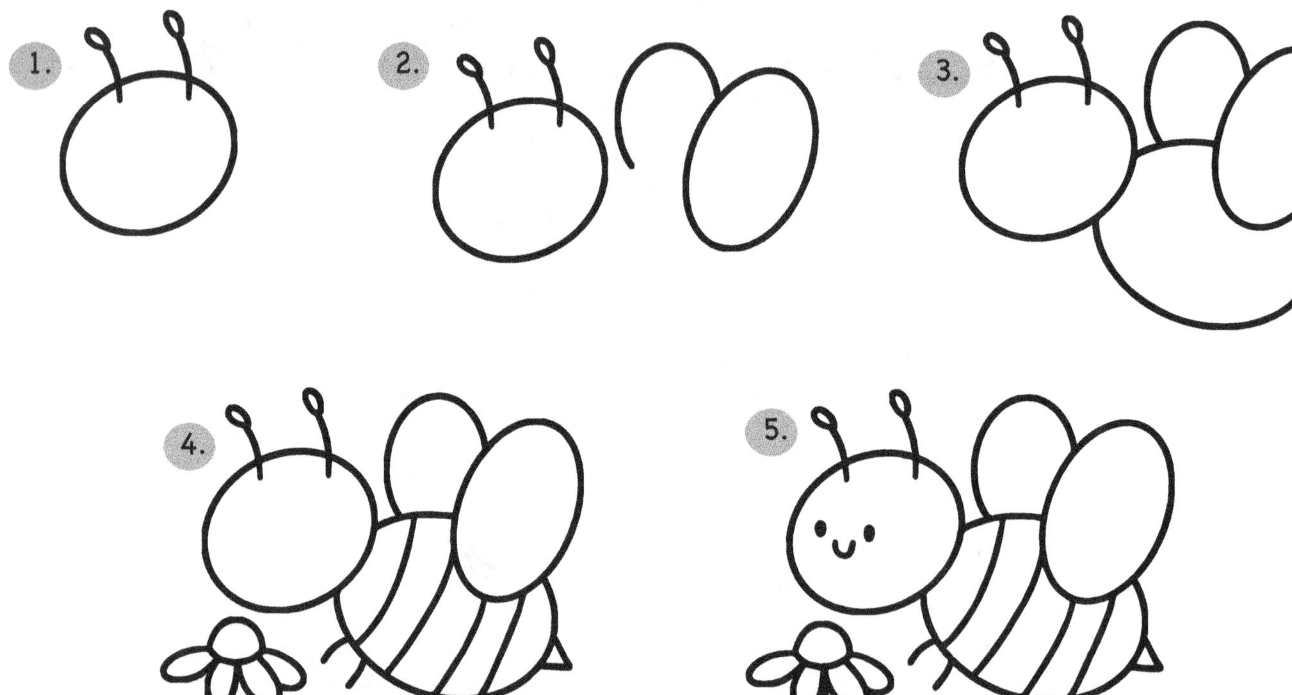

Practice for drawing here.

Snail

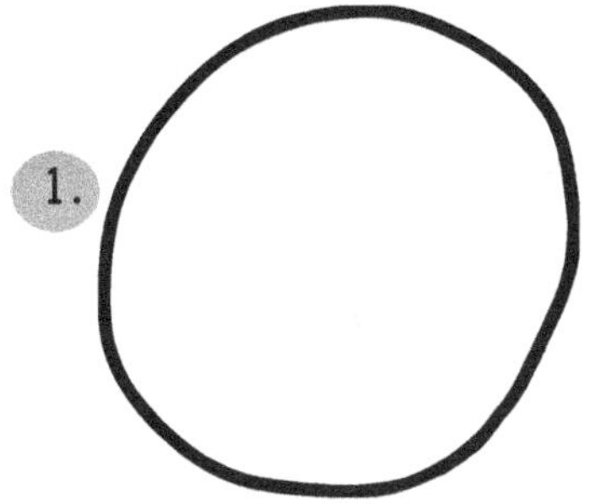

1.

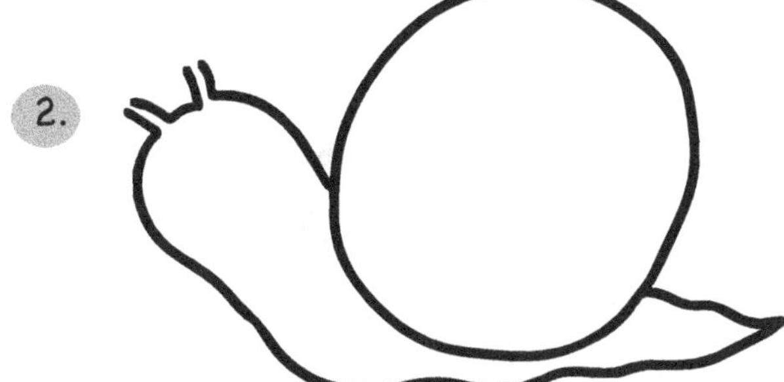

2.

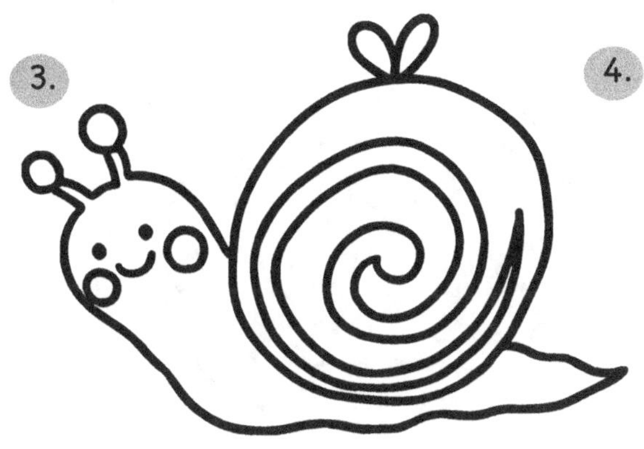

3.

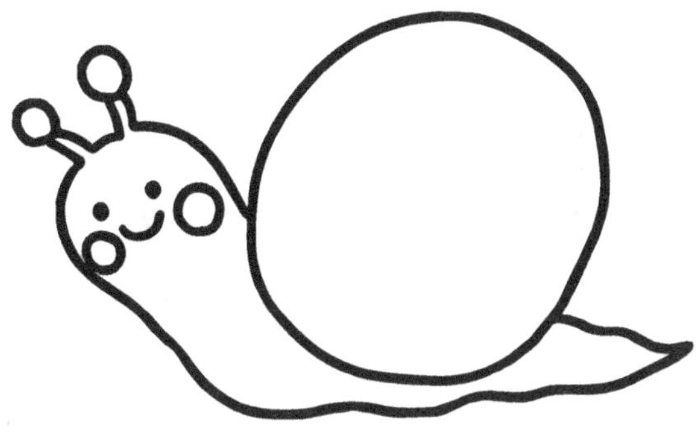

4.

Practice for drawing here.

Ladybug

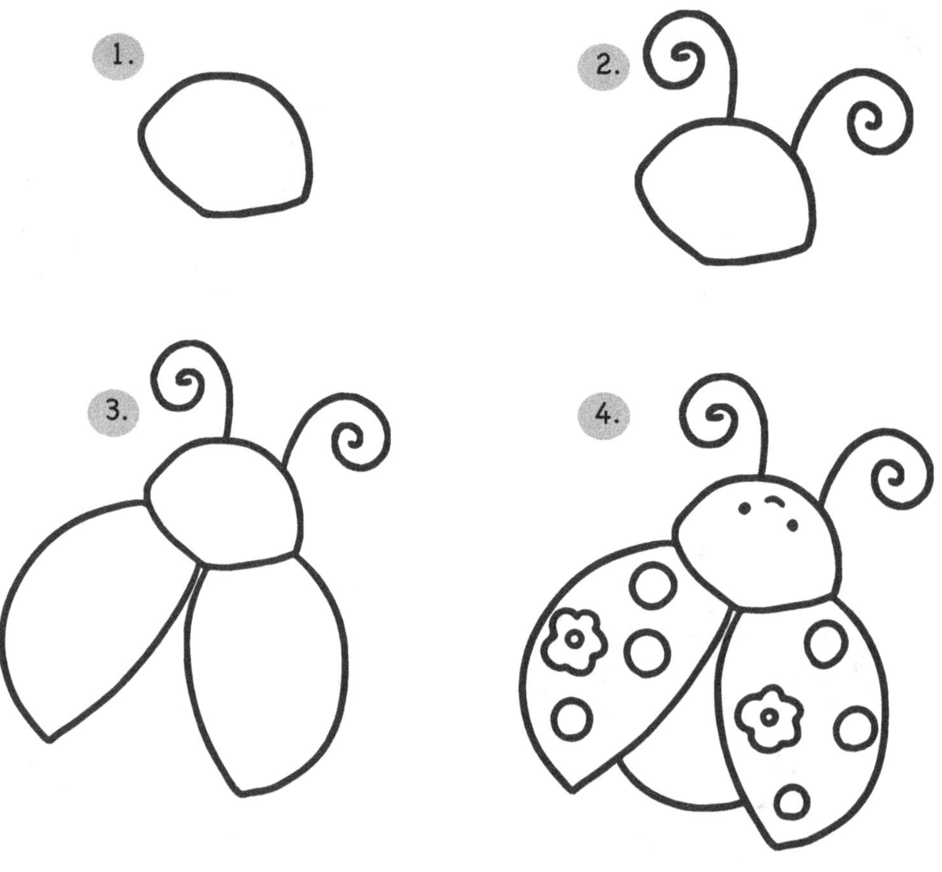

1.
2.
3.
4.

Practice for drawing here.

Mail Bird

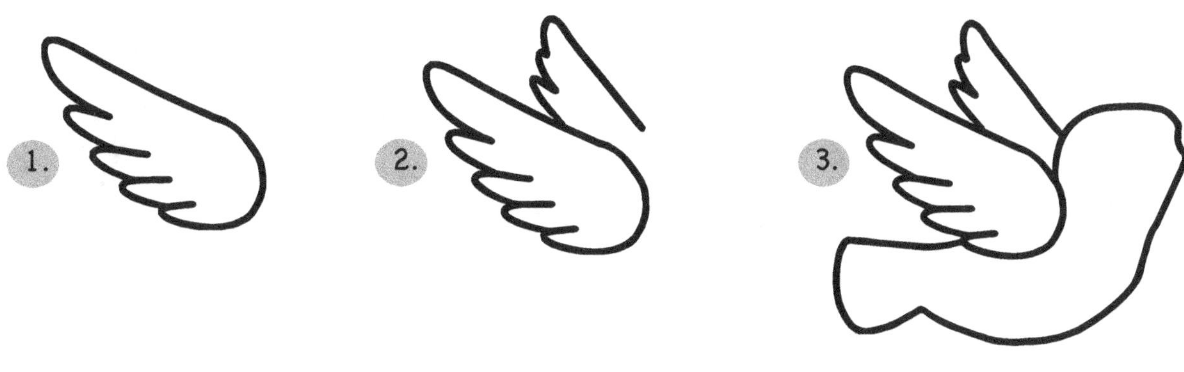

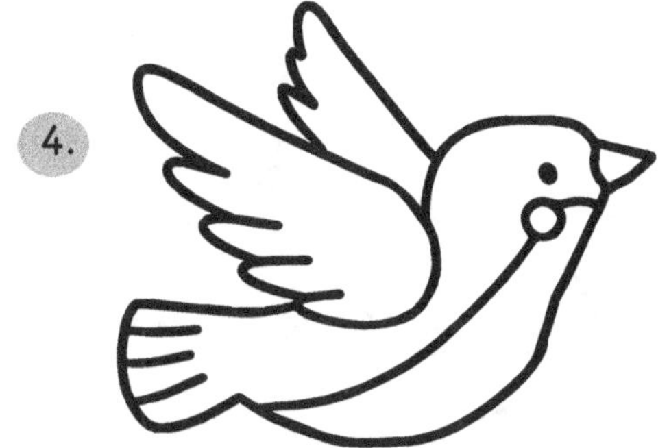

Practice for drawing here.

Watermelon

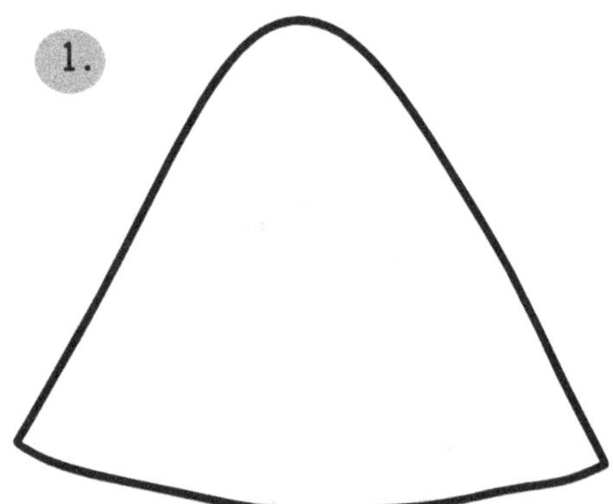

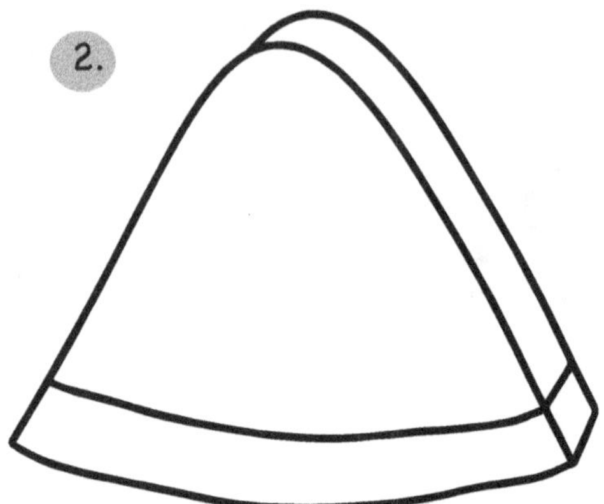

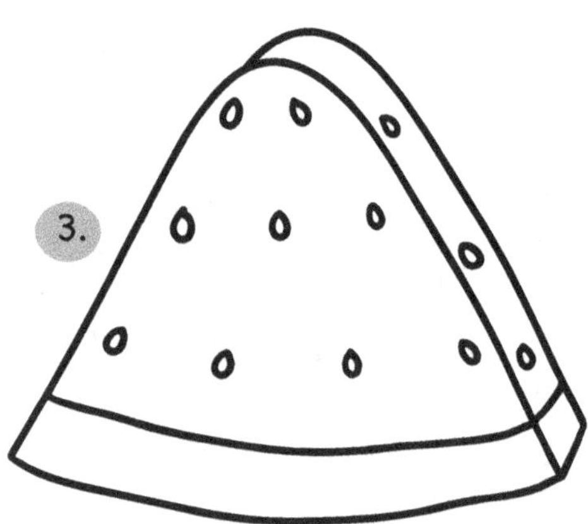

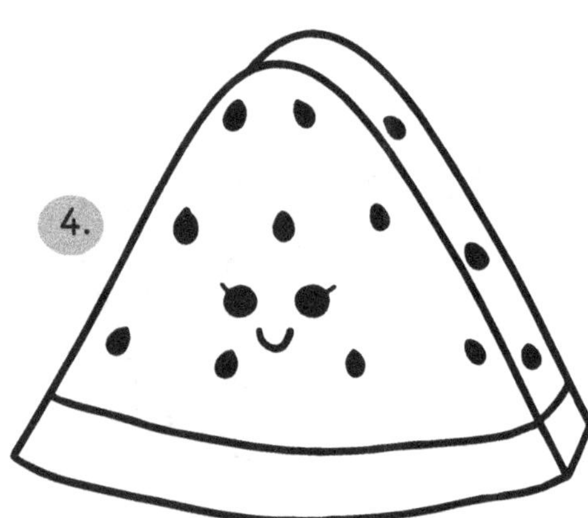

Practice for drawing here.

Tomato

 1.

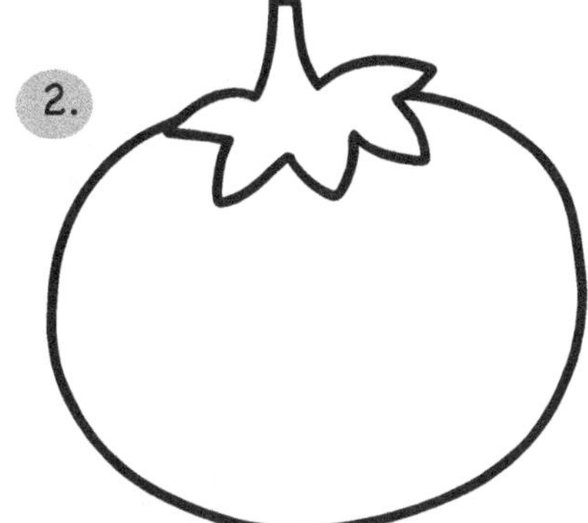 2.

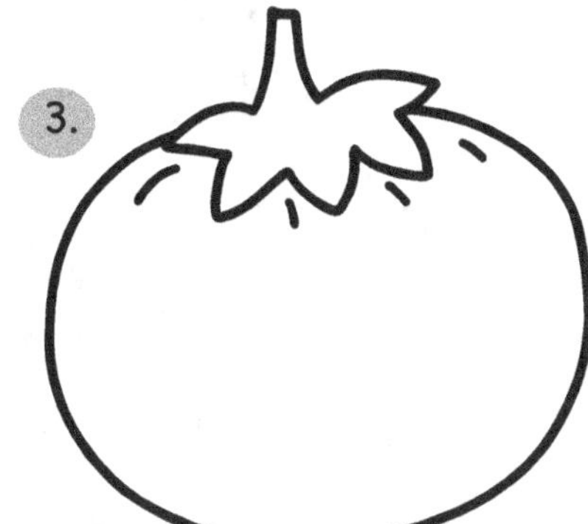 3.

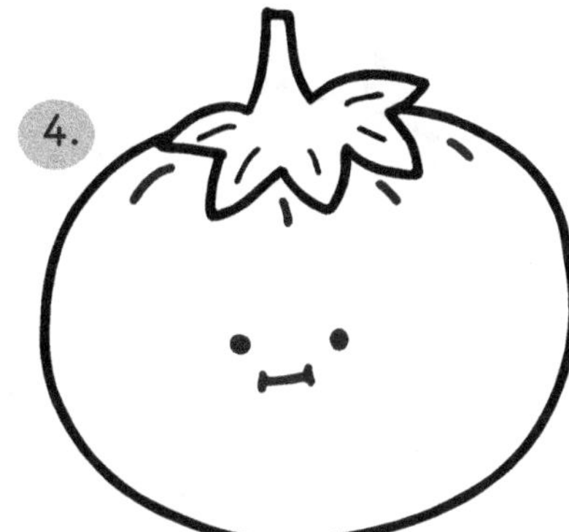 4.

Practice for drawing here.

Strawberry

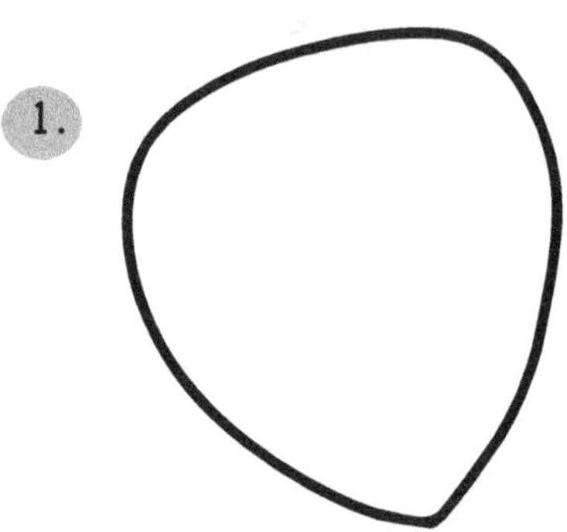

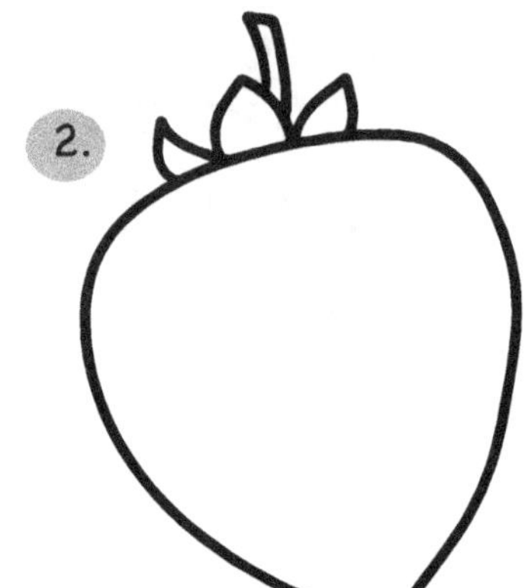

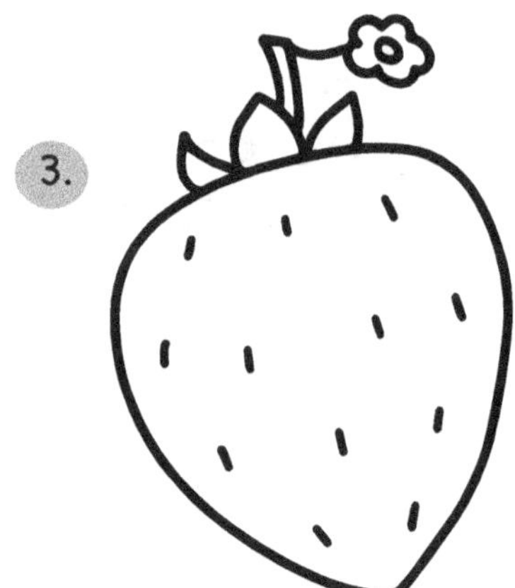

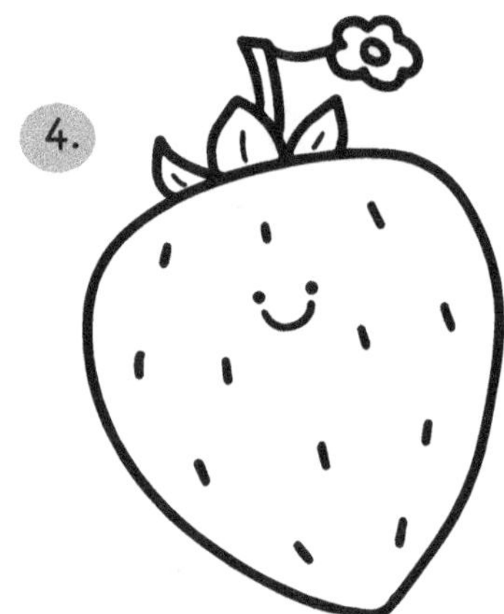

Practice for drawing here.

Pumpkin

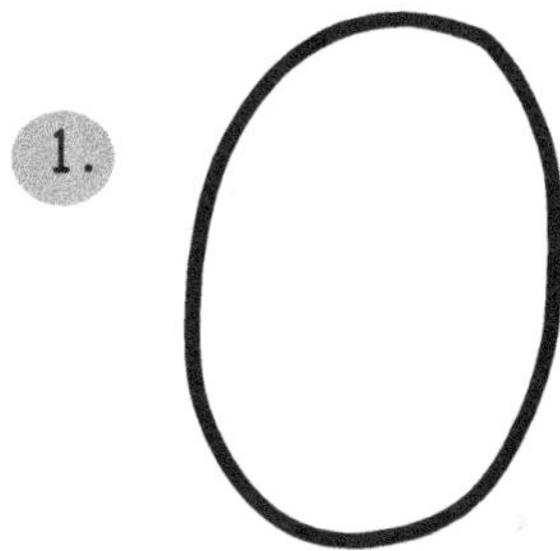

1.

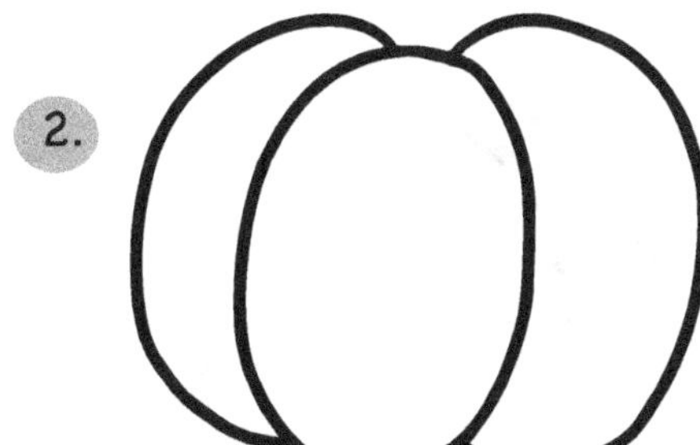

2.

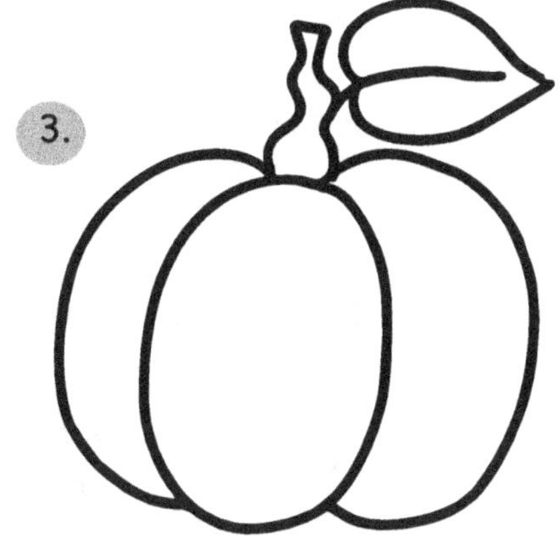

3.

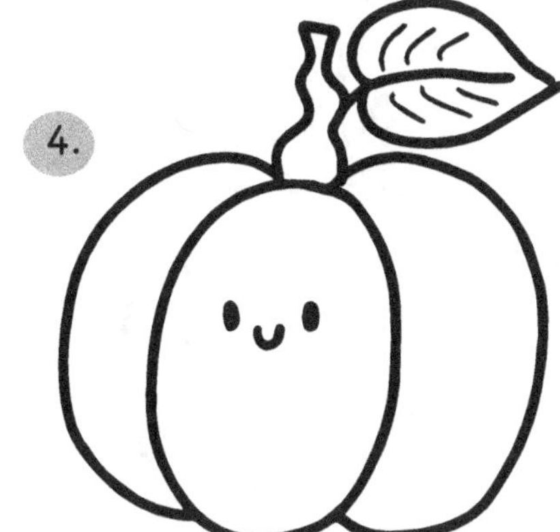

4.

Practice for drawing here.

Pineapple

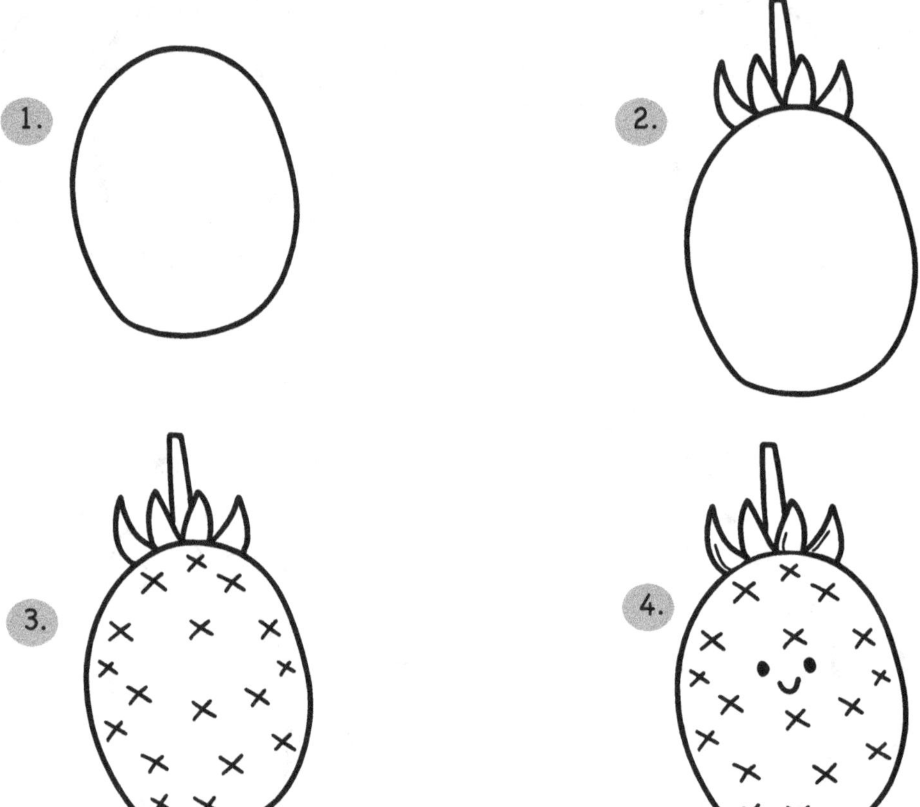

Practice for drawing here.

16.

Peas

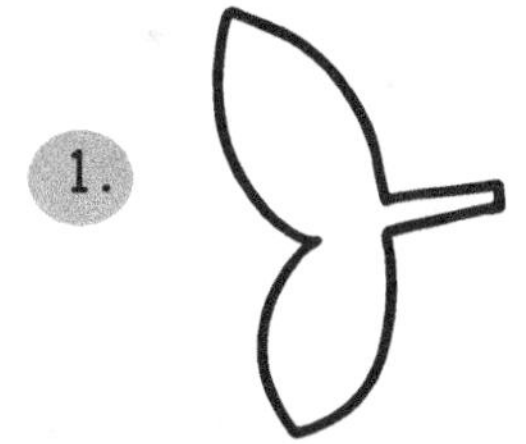

1.

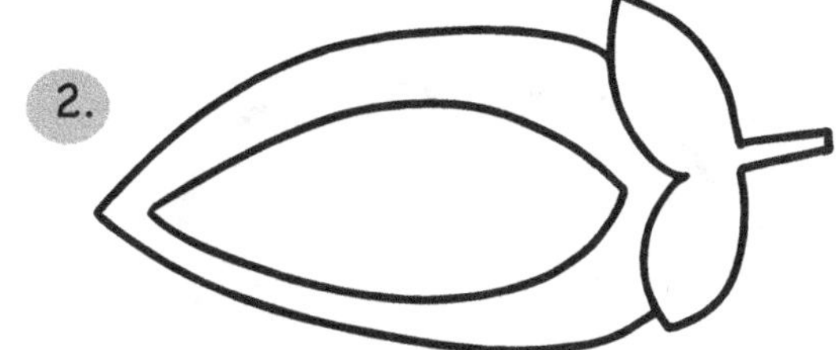

2.

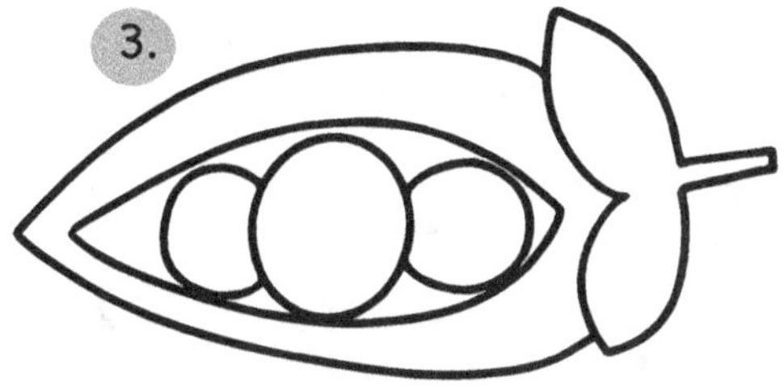

3.

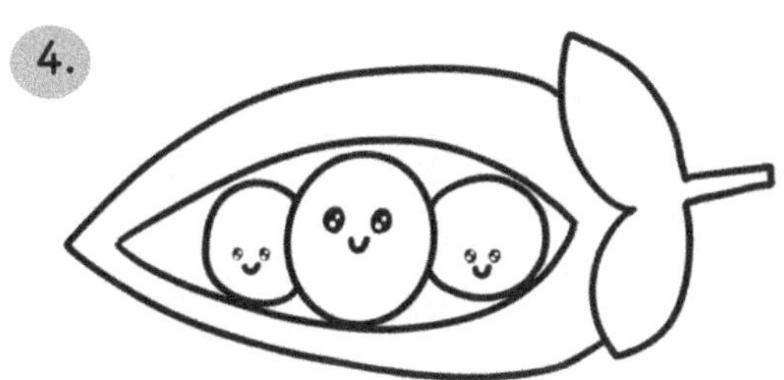

4.

Practice for drawing here.

Peach

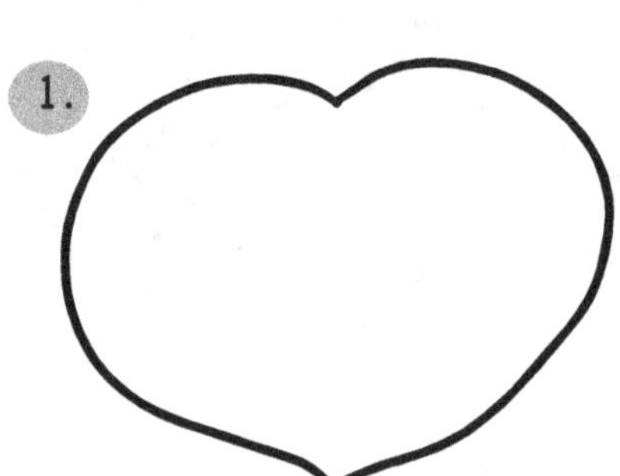

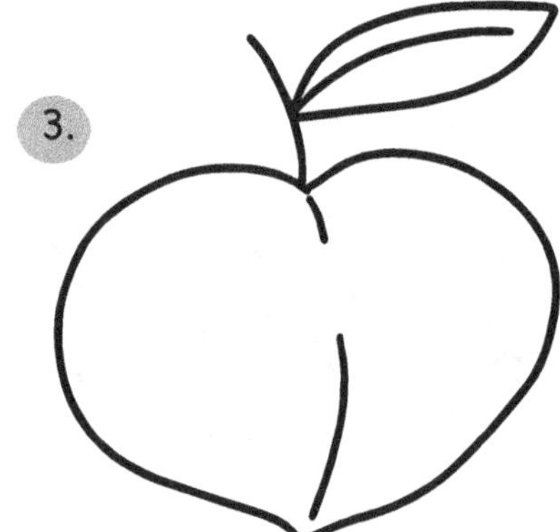

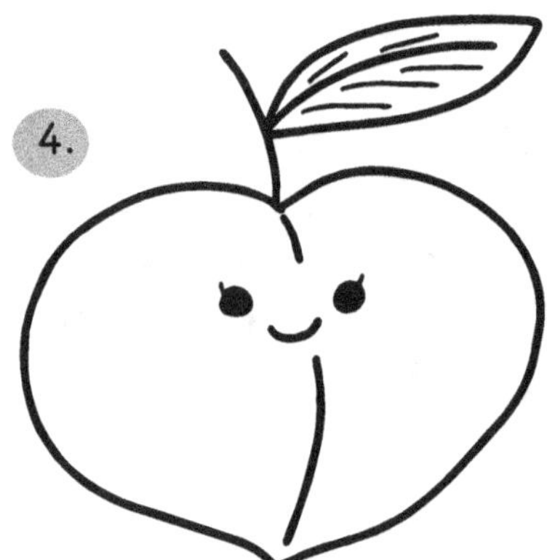

Practice for drawing here.

Orange

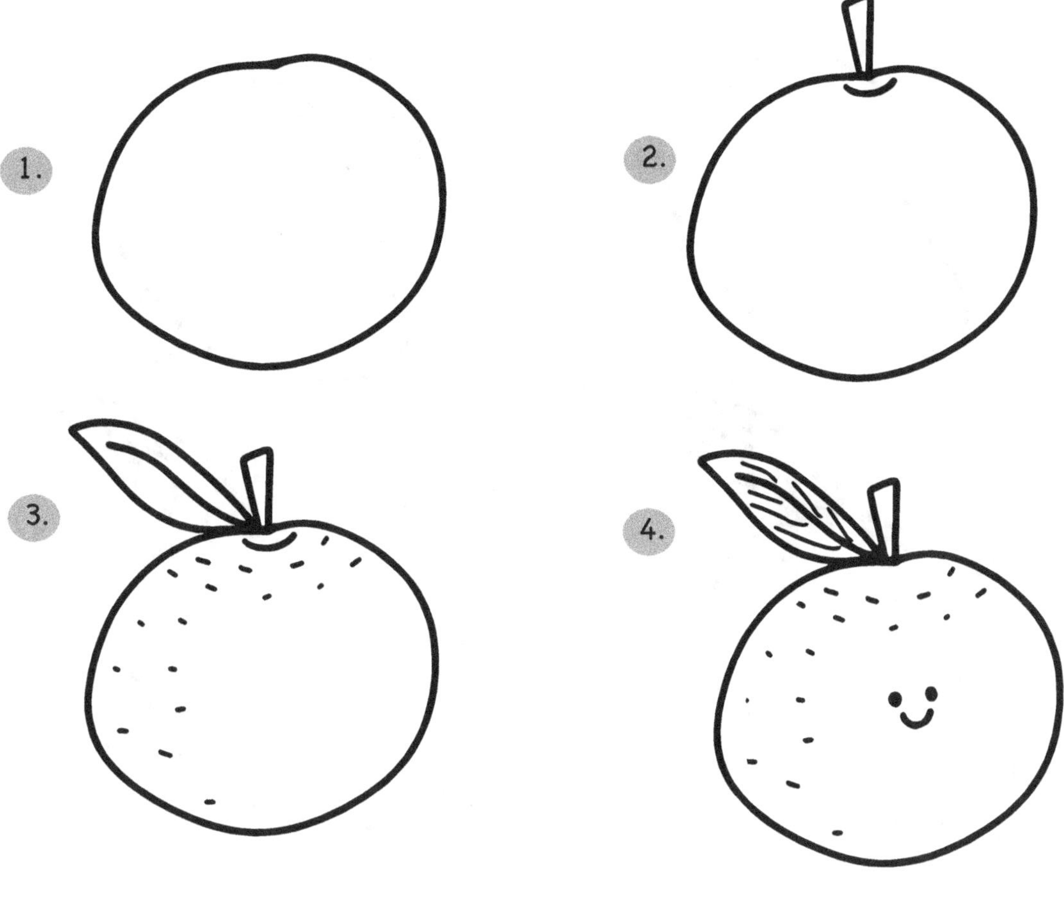

Practice for drawing here.

Mango

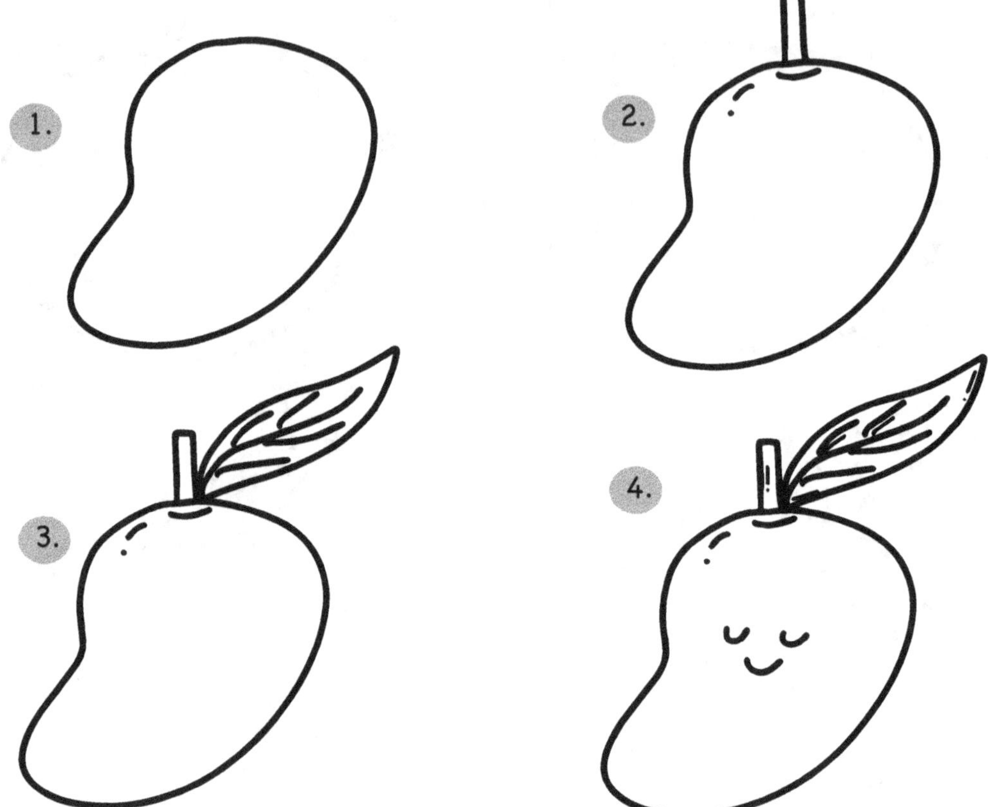

Practice for drawing here.

Cherry

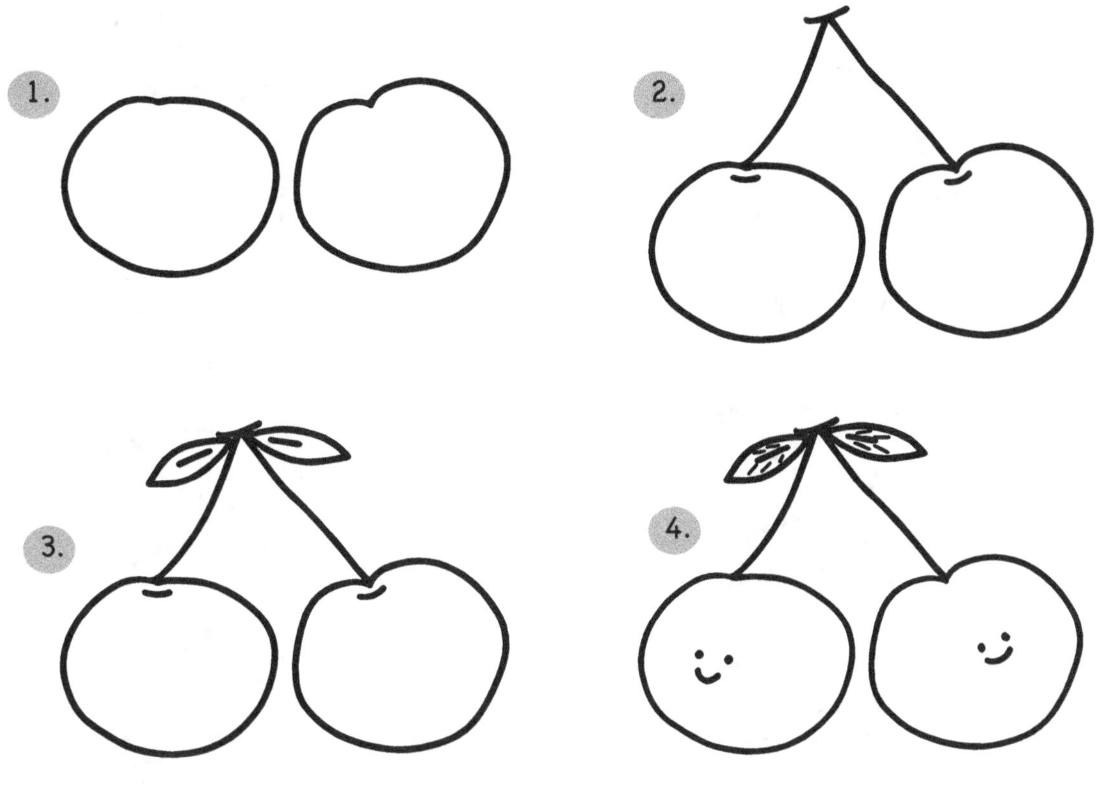

Practice for drawing here.

Carrot

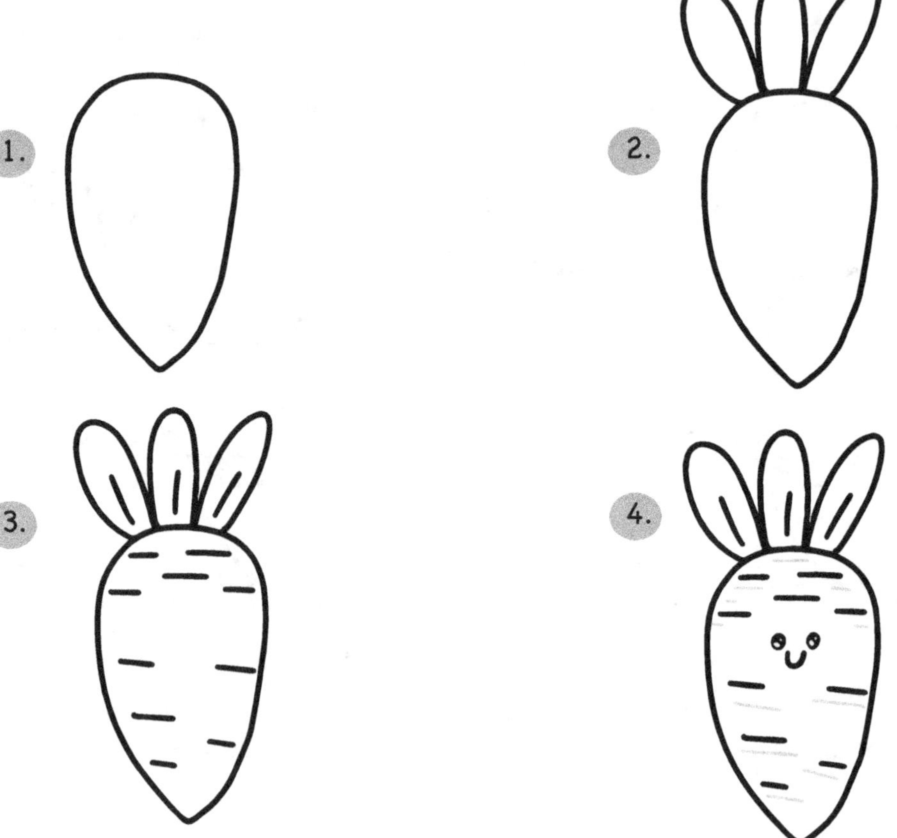

Blueberry

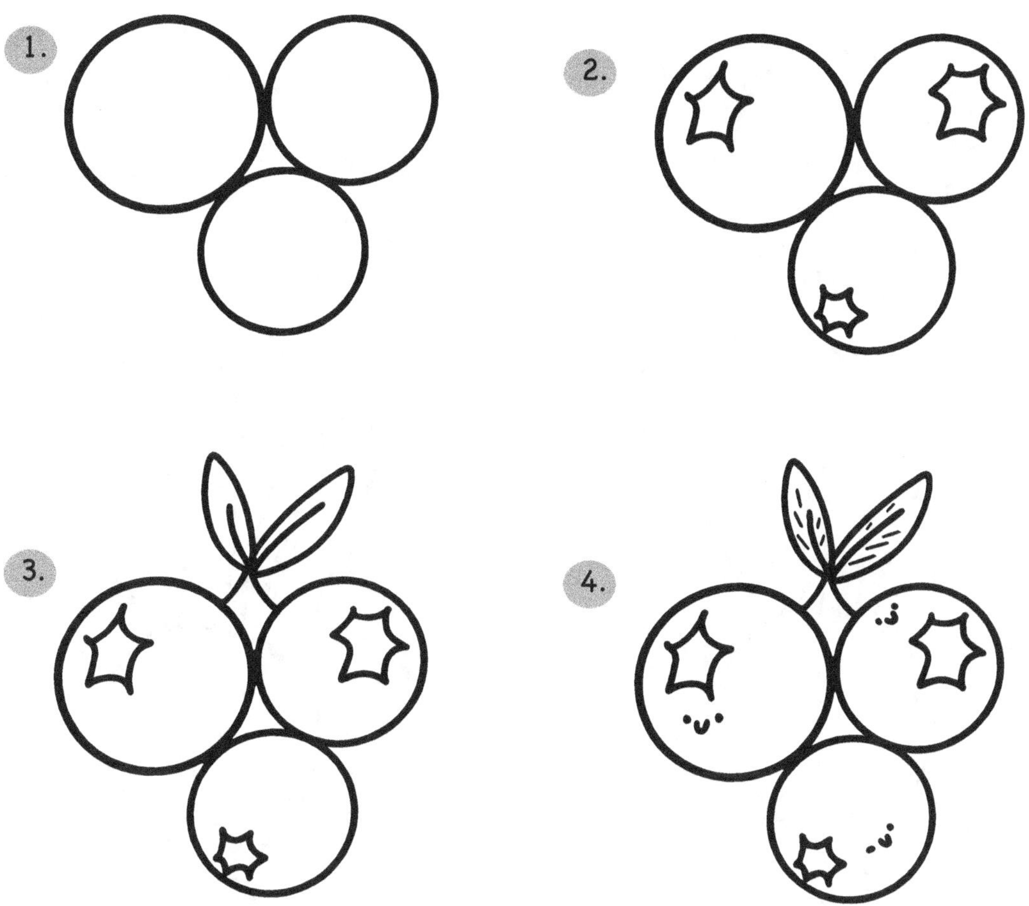

Practice for drawing here.

Beetroot

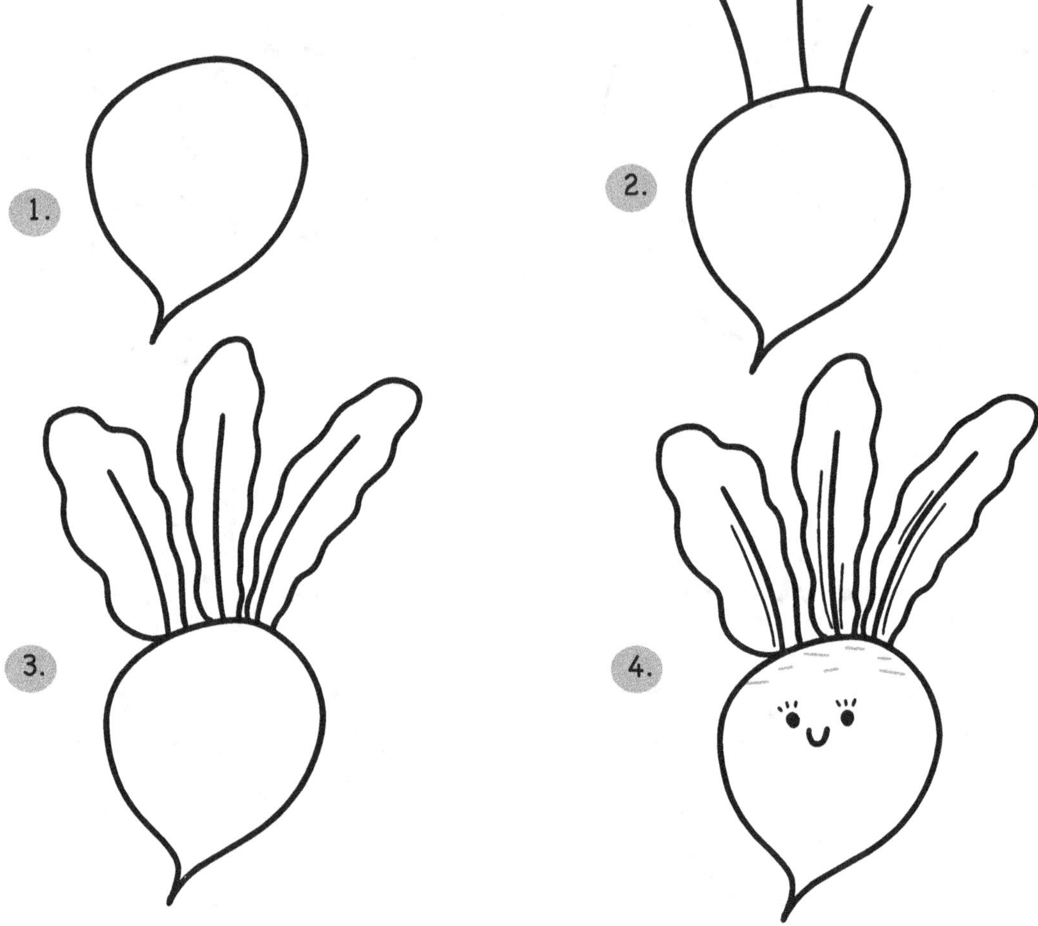

Avocondo

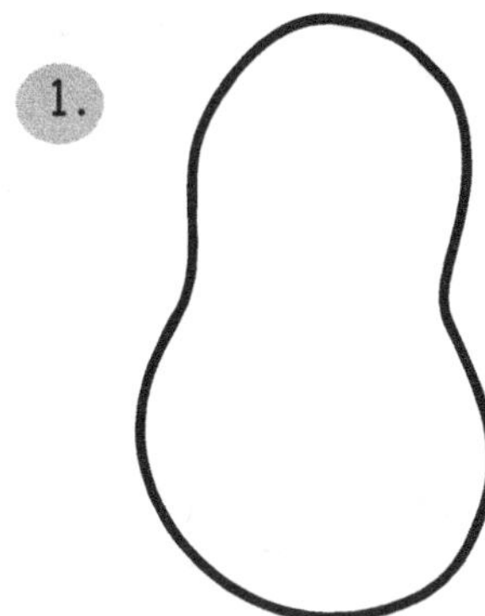

1.

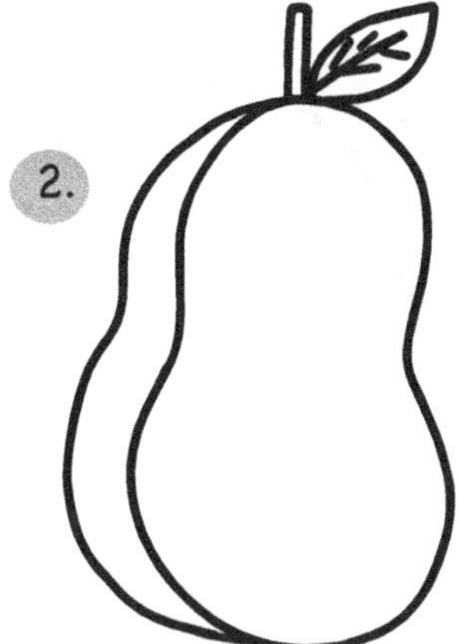

2.

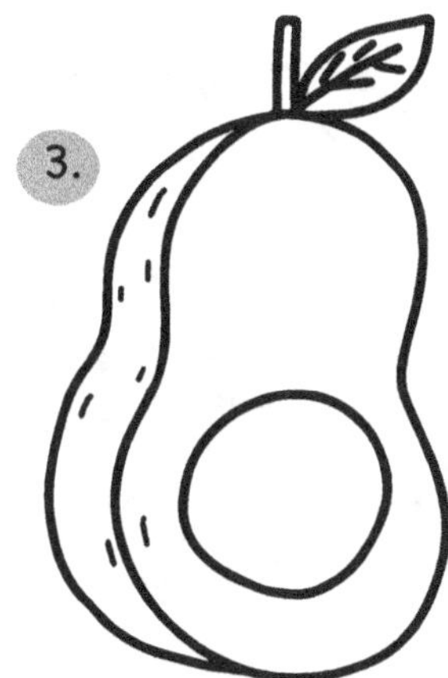

3.

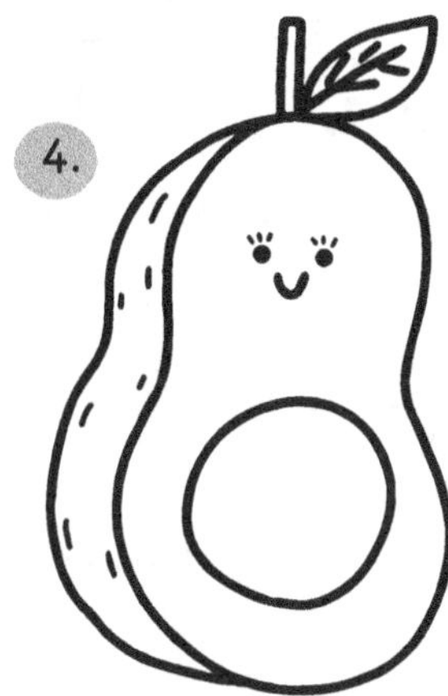

4.

Practice for drawing here.

An apple

1.

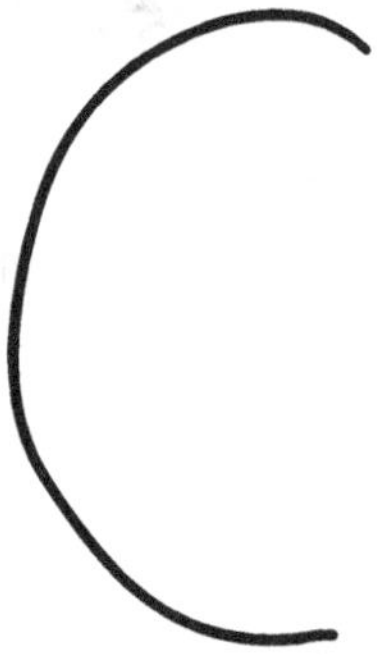

2.

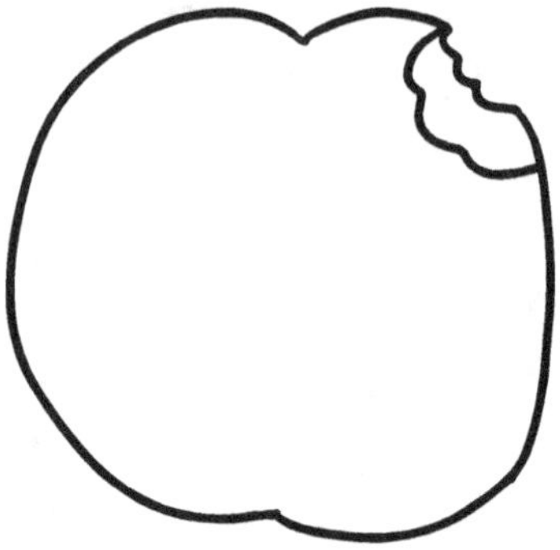

3.

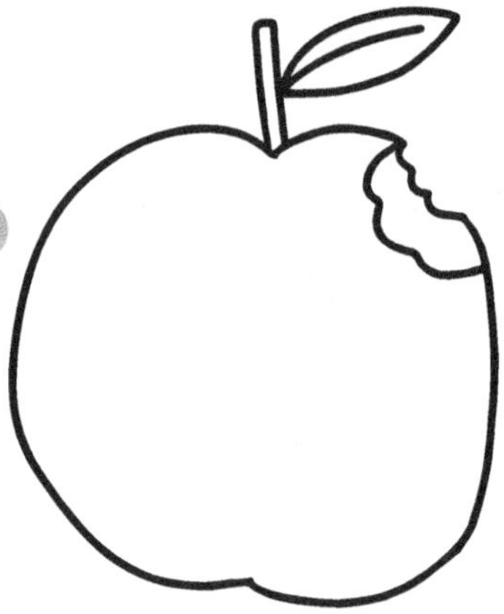

4.

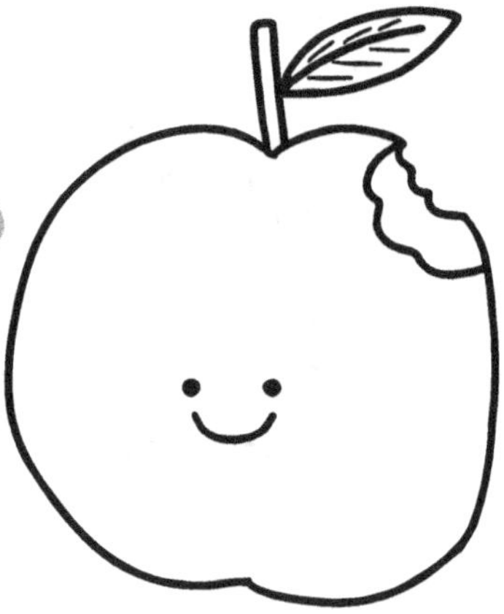

Practice for drawing here.

Onion

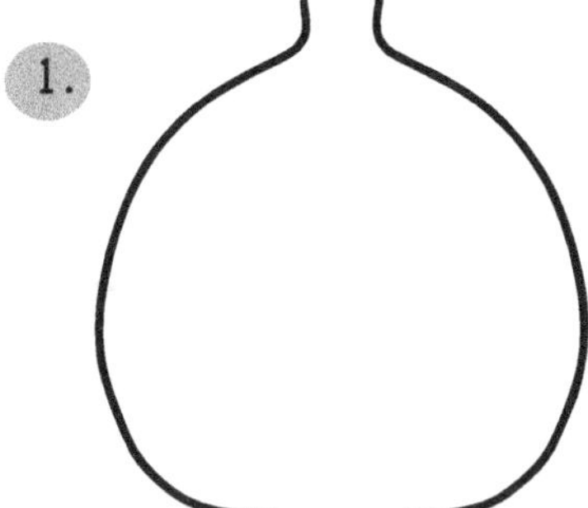

1.

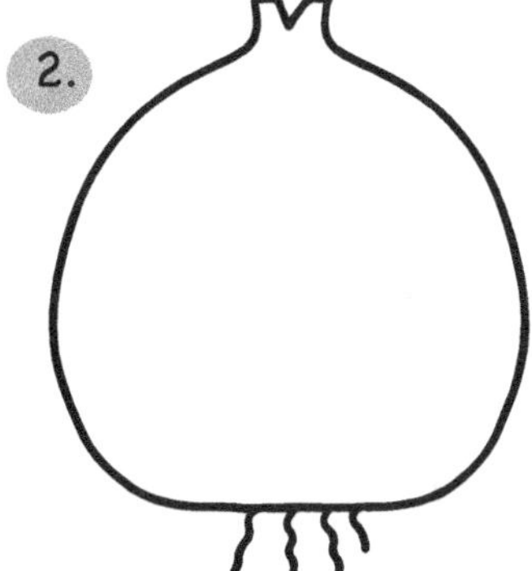

2.

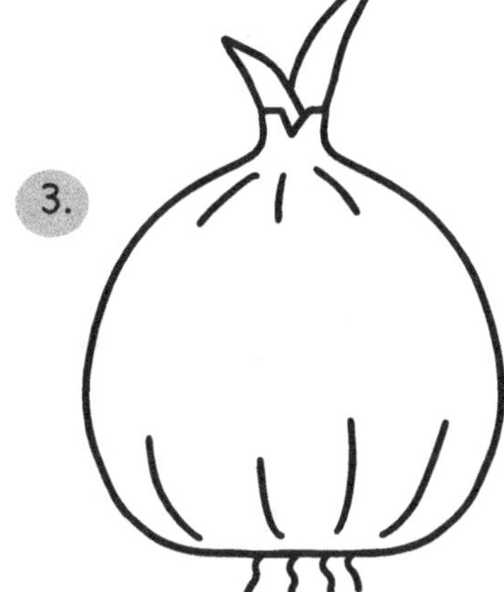

3.

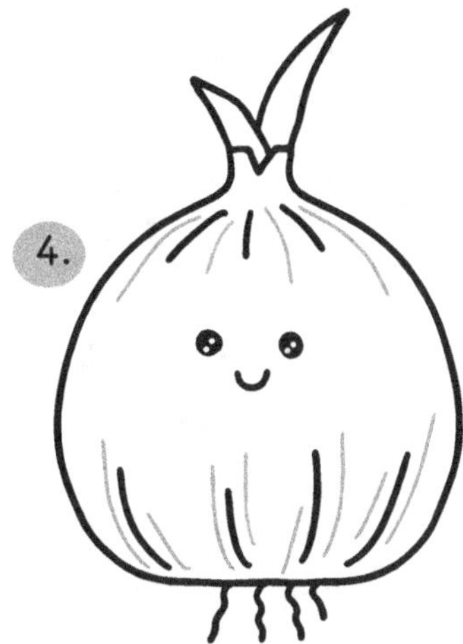

4.

Practice for drawing here.

Mushroom

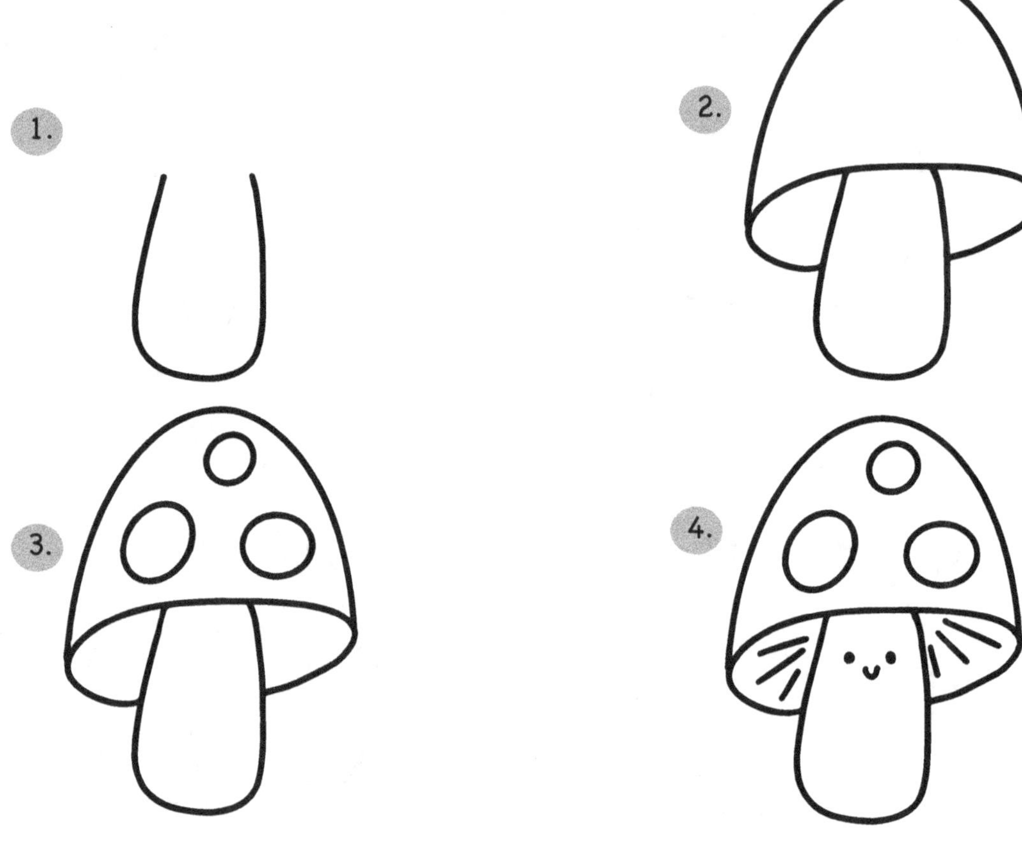

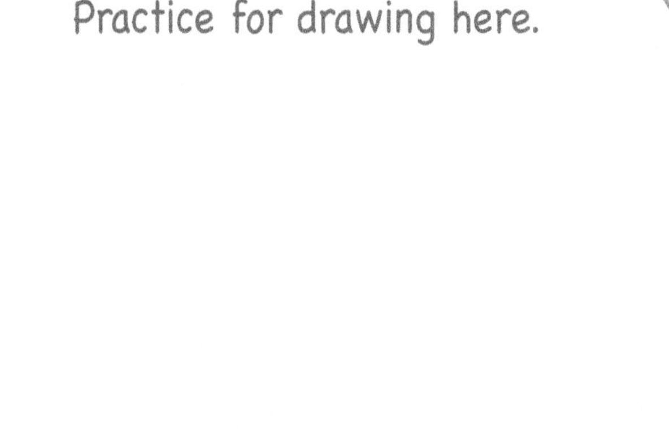

Lemon

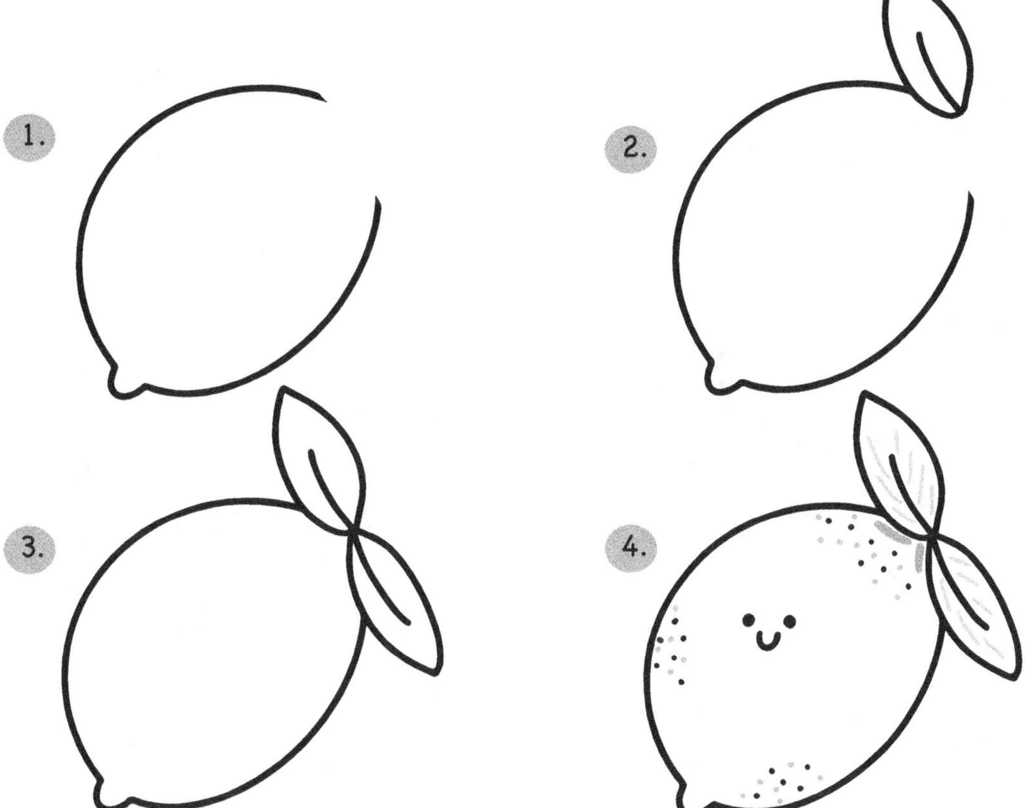

1.
2.
3.
4.

Practice for drawing here.

Chili

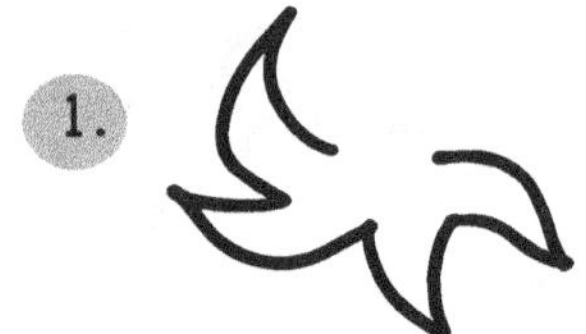

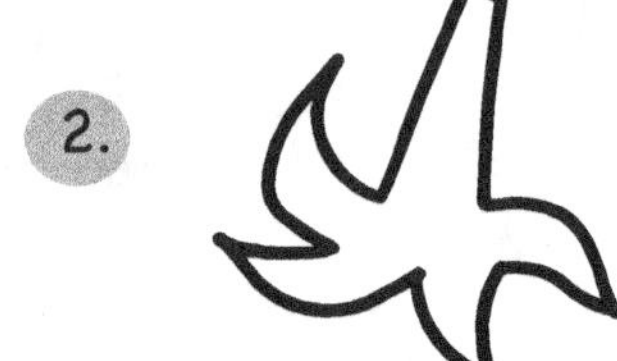

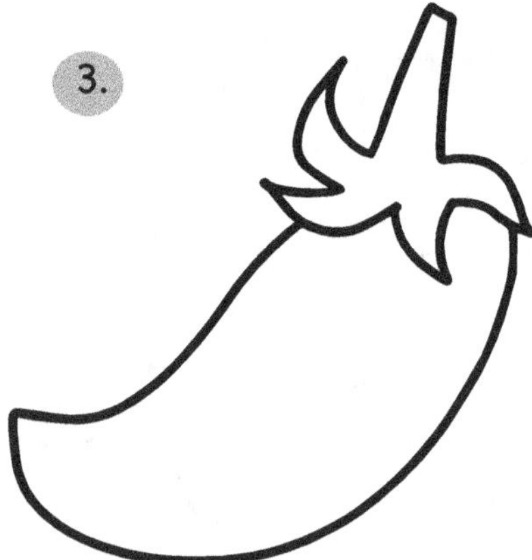

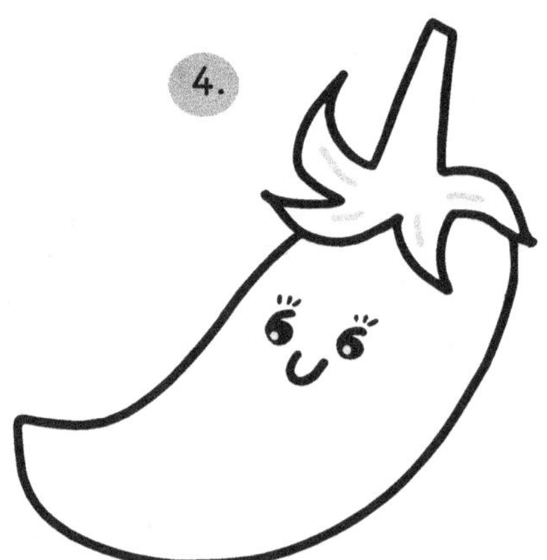

Practice for drawing here.

Broccoli

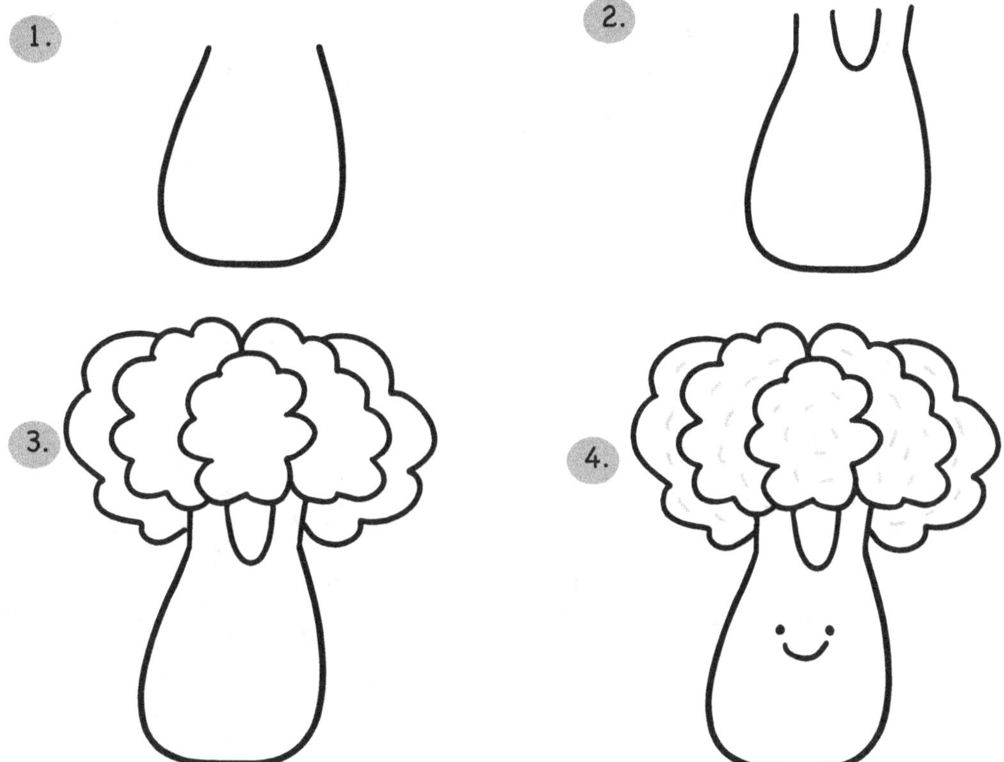

Practice for drawing here.

Waffle

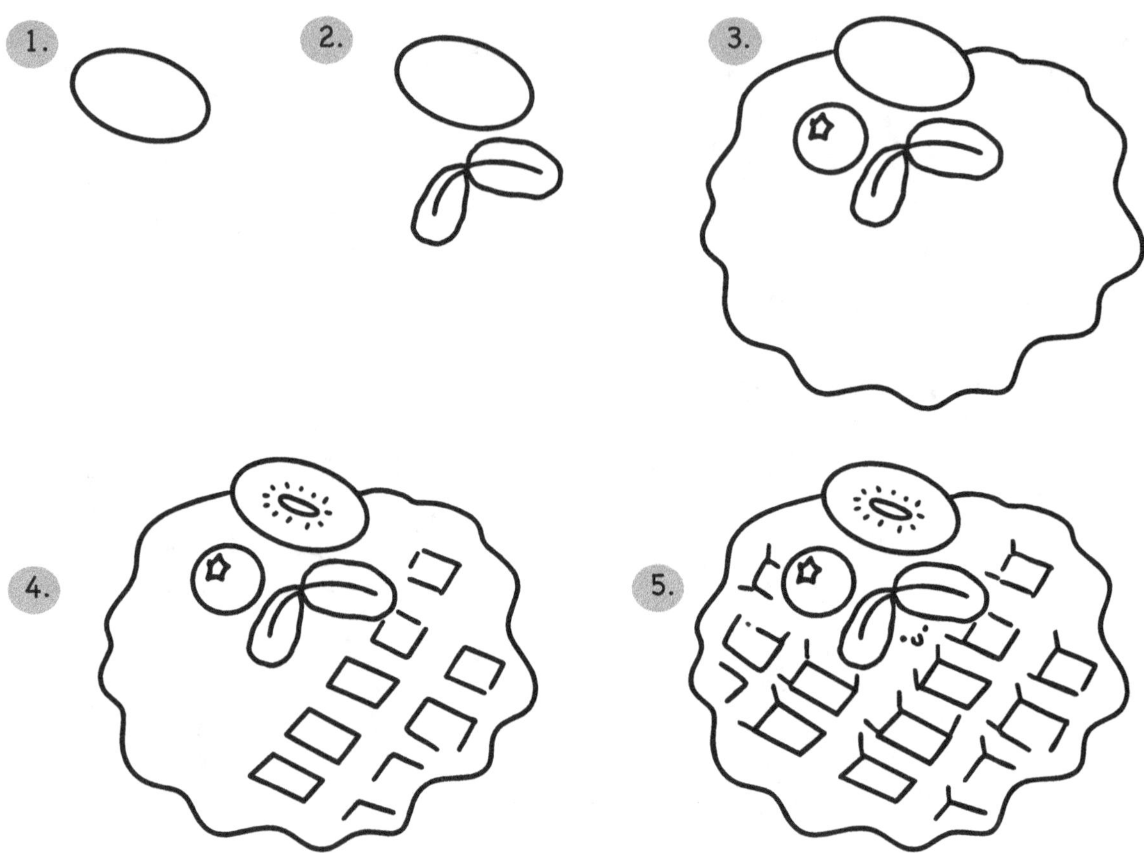

Practice for drawing here.

Crepes

1.

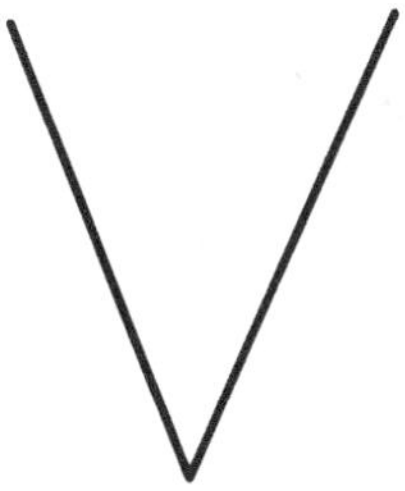

2.

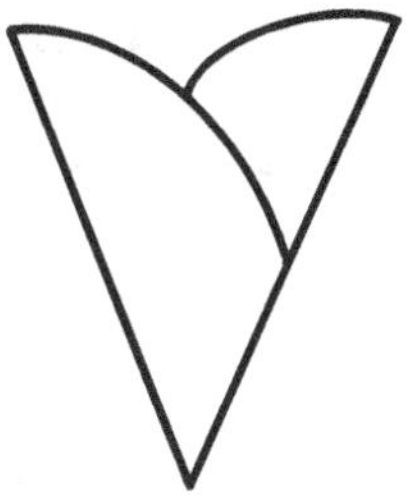

3.

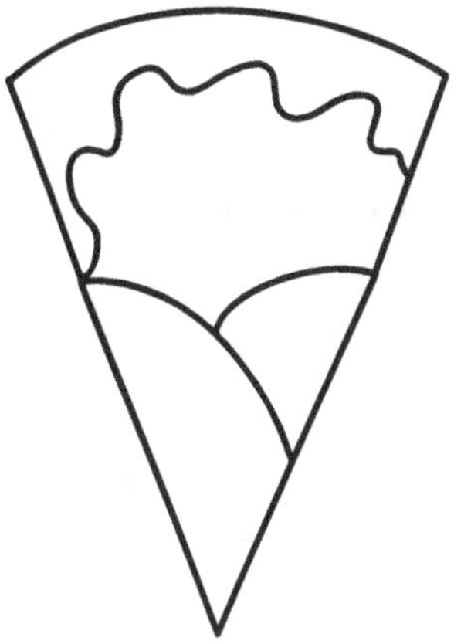

4.

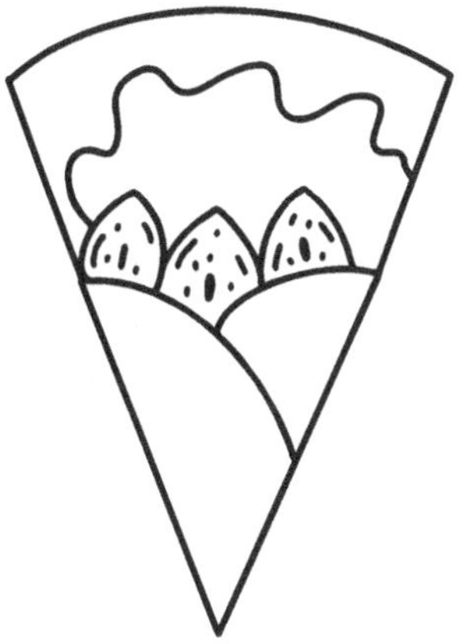

5.

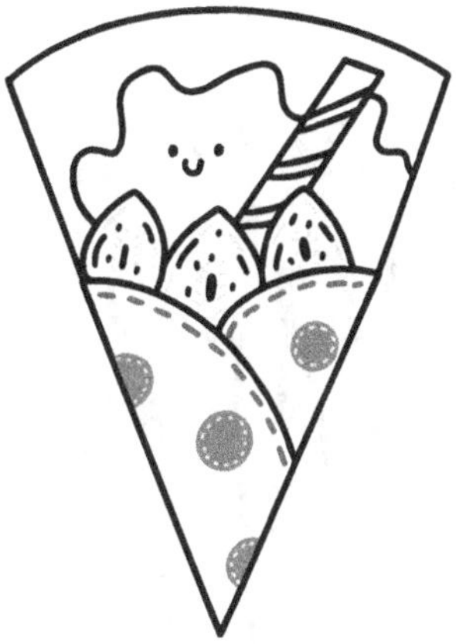

Practice for drawing here.

French fries

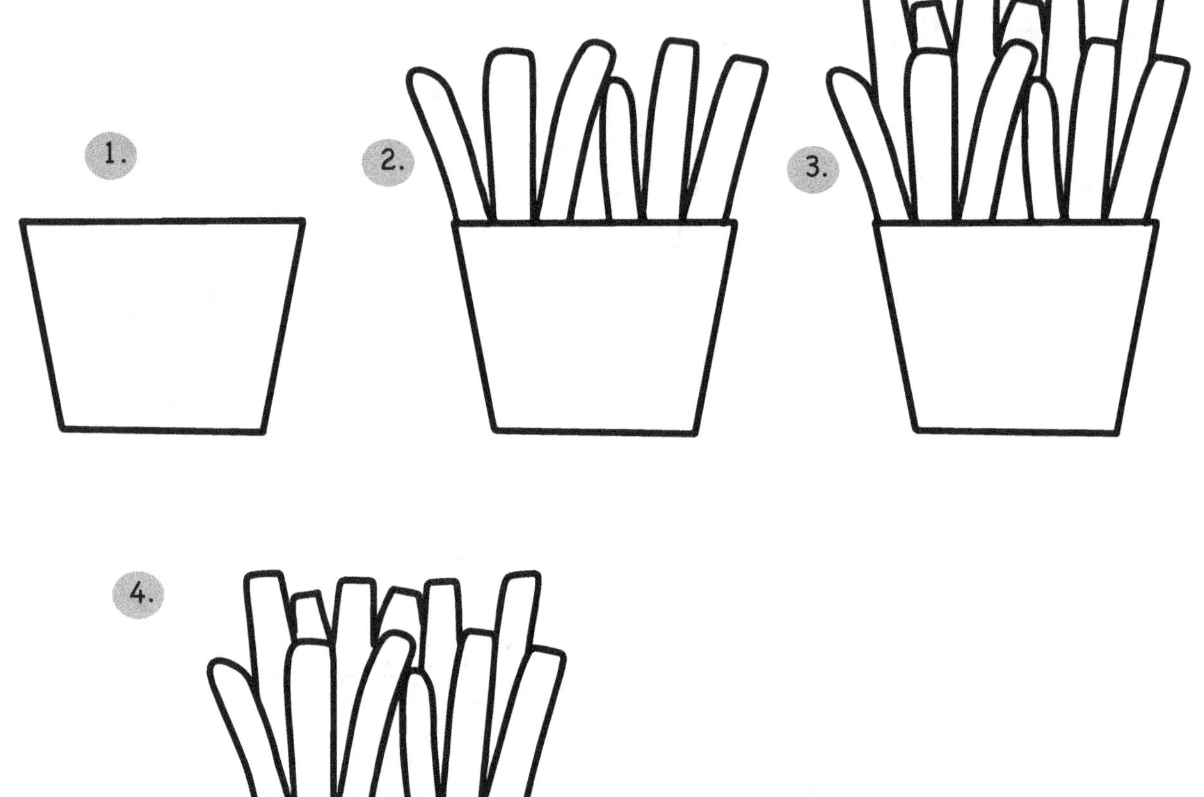

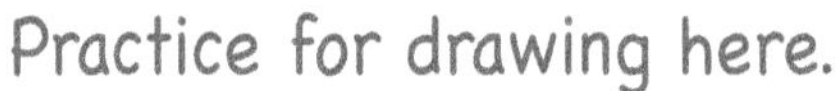

Cherry Pie

1.

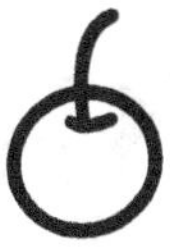

2.

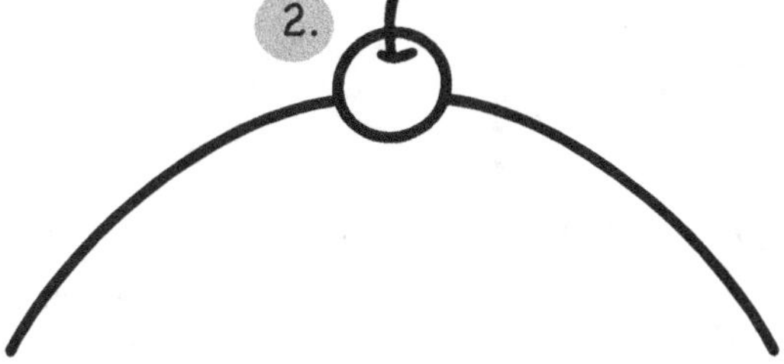

3.

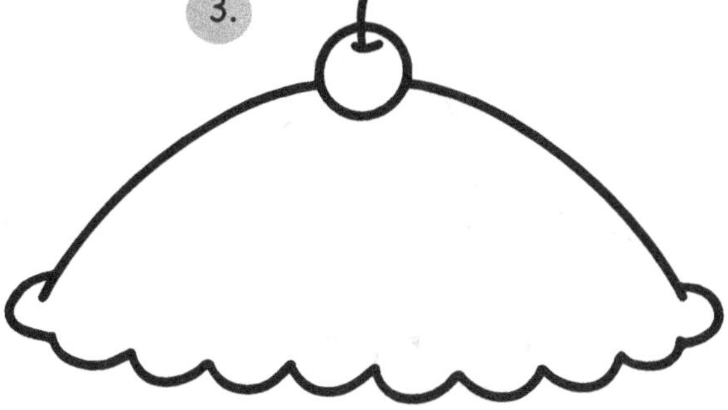

4.

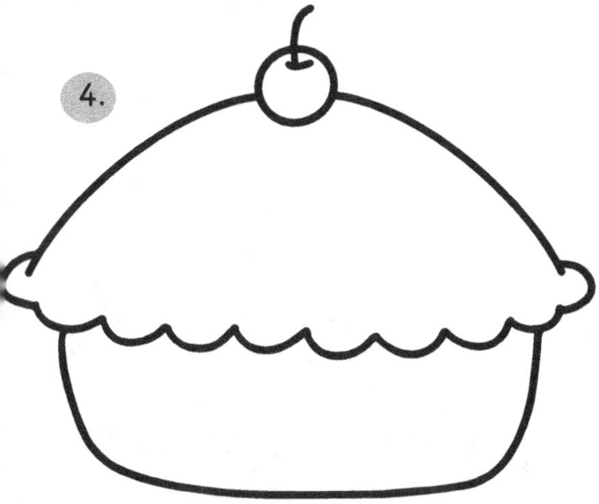

5.

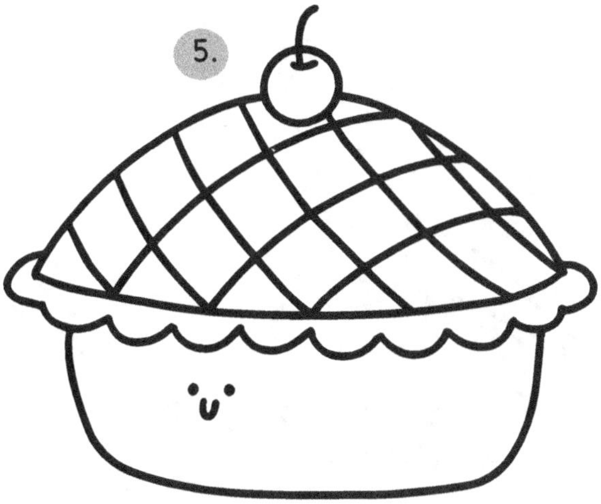

Strawberry Cheesecake

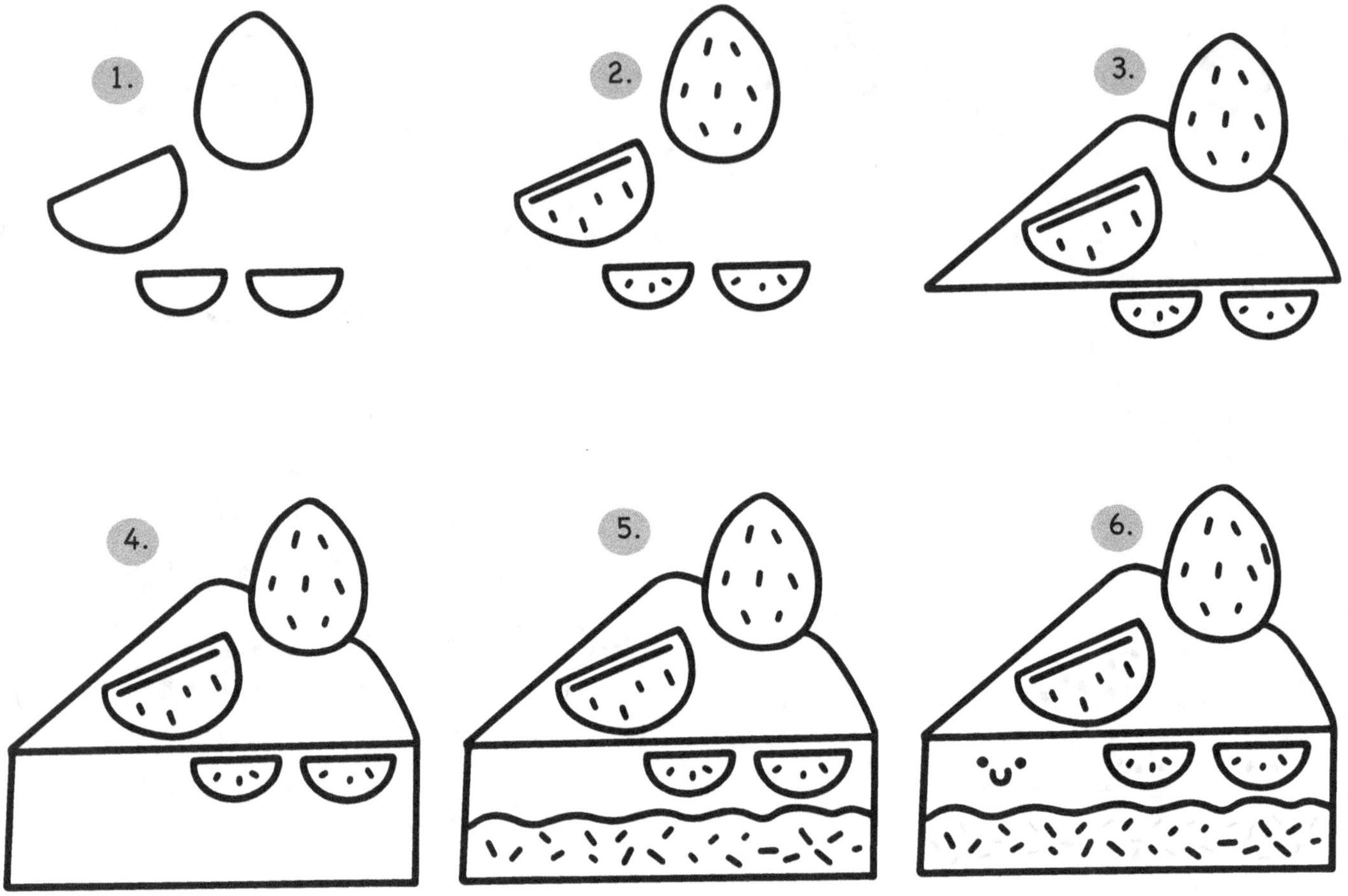

1.

2.

3.

4.

5.

6.

Practice for drawing here.

Pudding

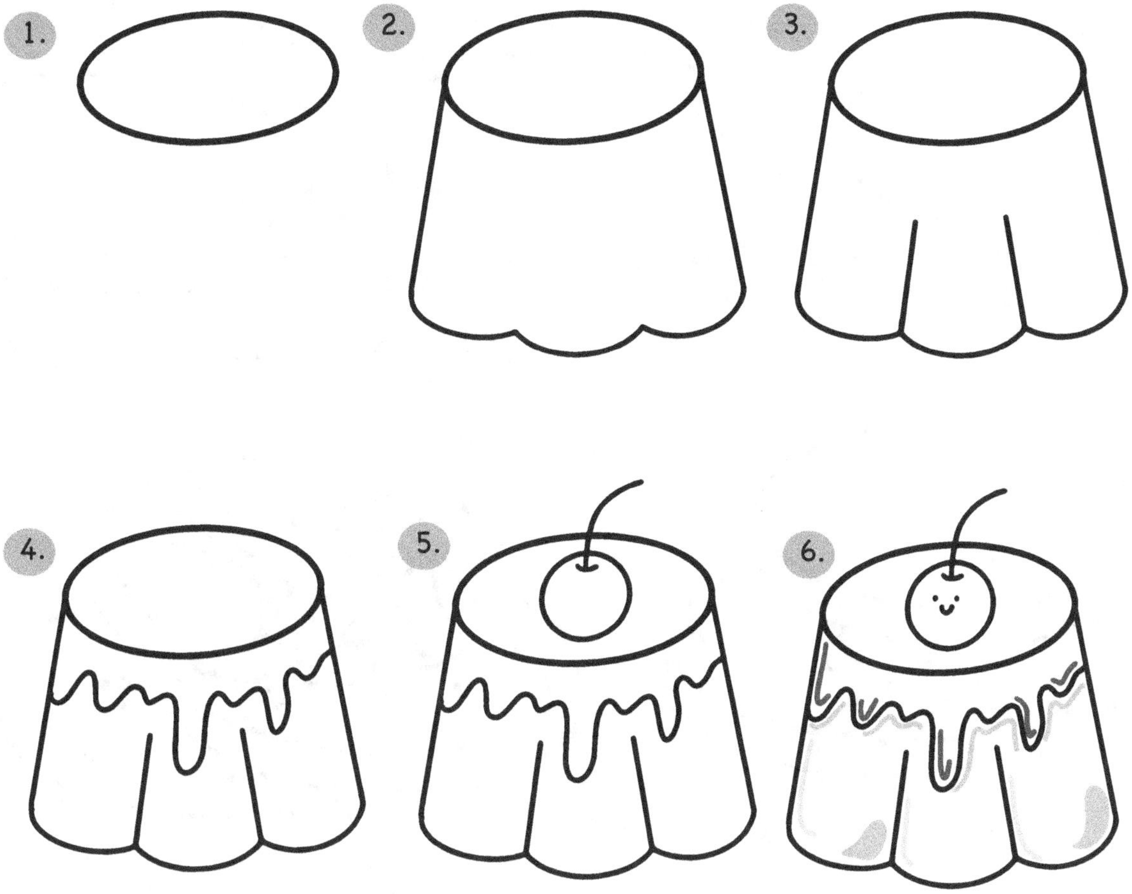

1. 2. 3.

4. 5. 6.

Practice for drawing here.

Pancakes

1.

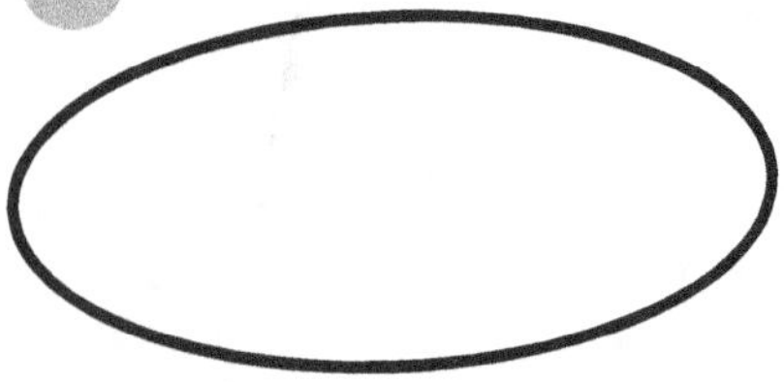

2.

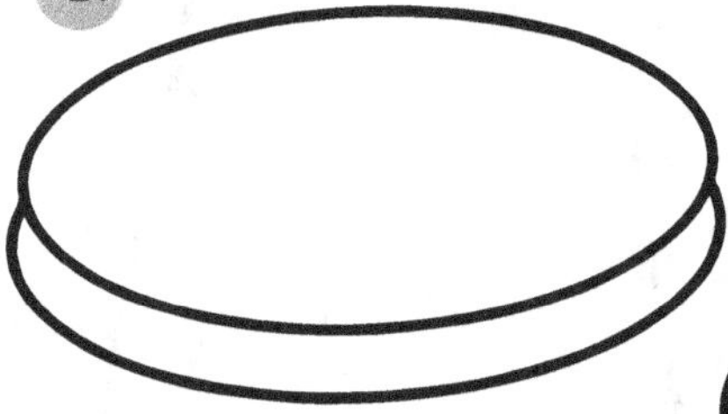

3.

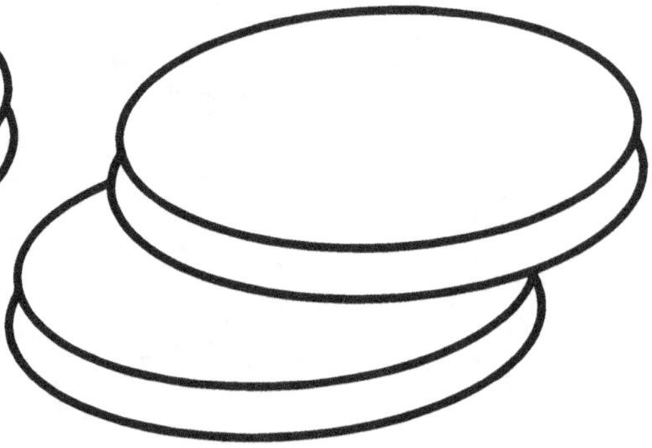

4.

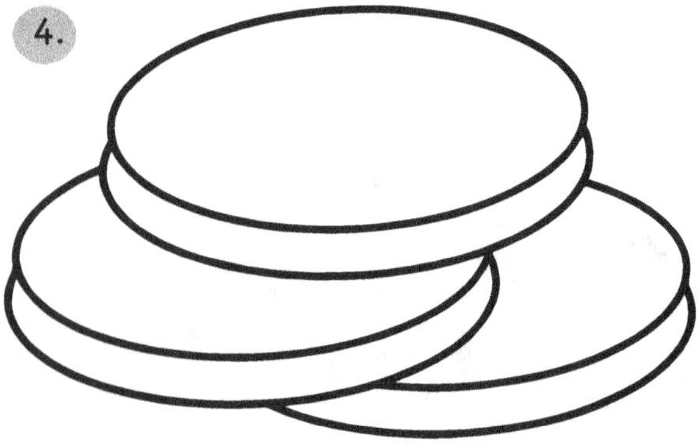

5.

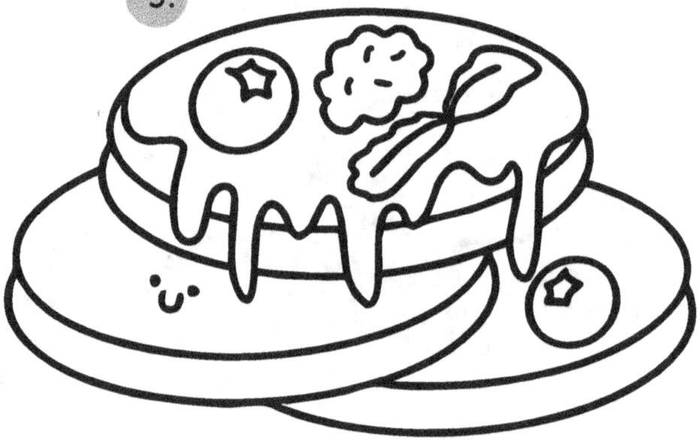

Practice for drawing here.

Croissant

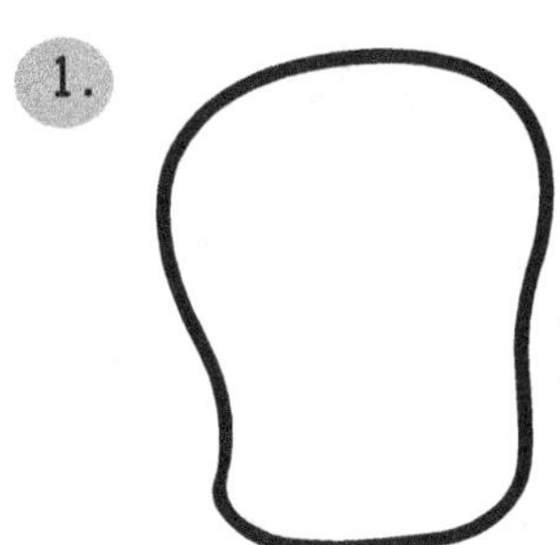

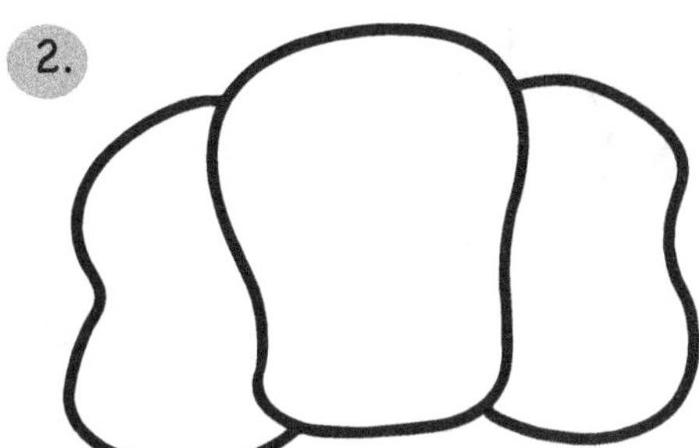

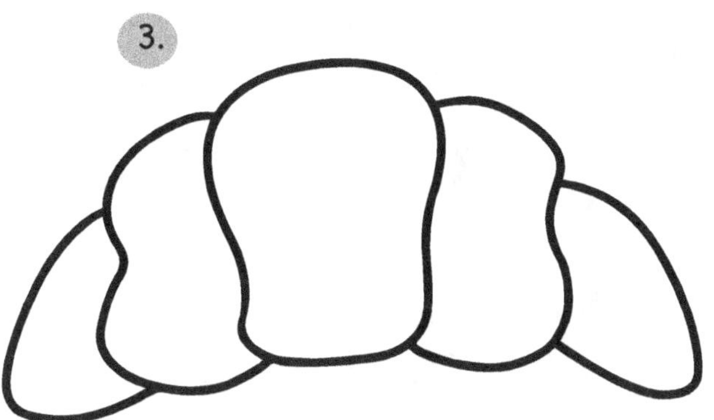

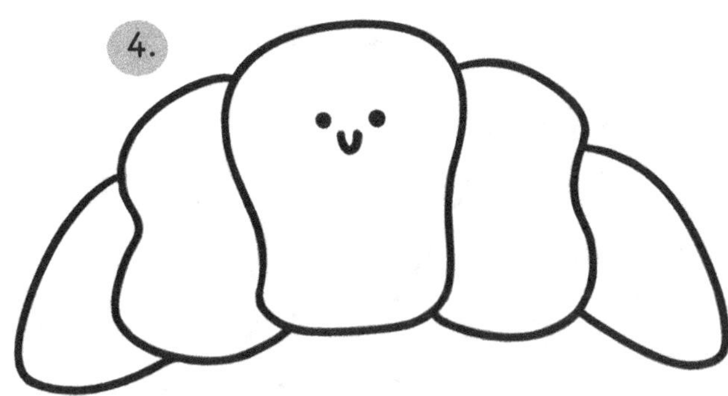

Practice for drawing here.

Cream soda

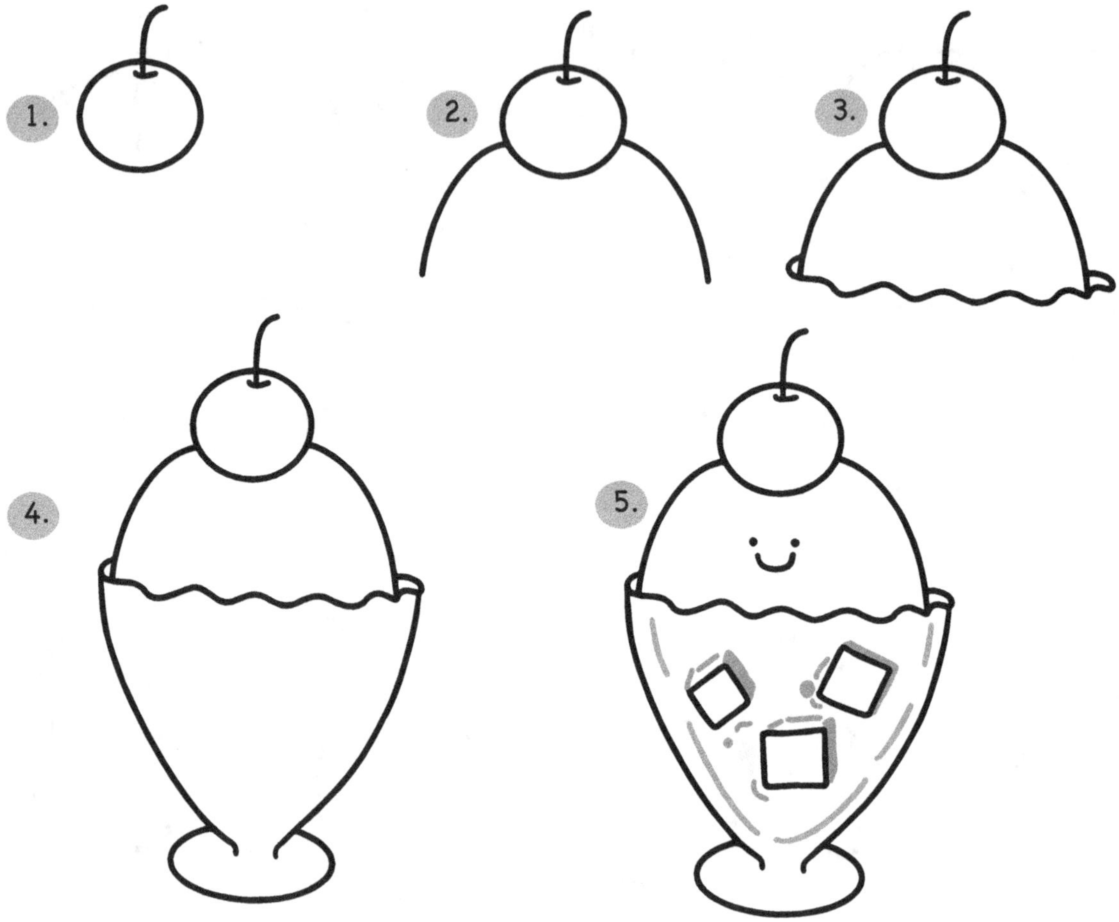

1.

2.

3.

4.

5.

Practice for drawing here.

Cupcake

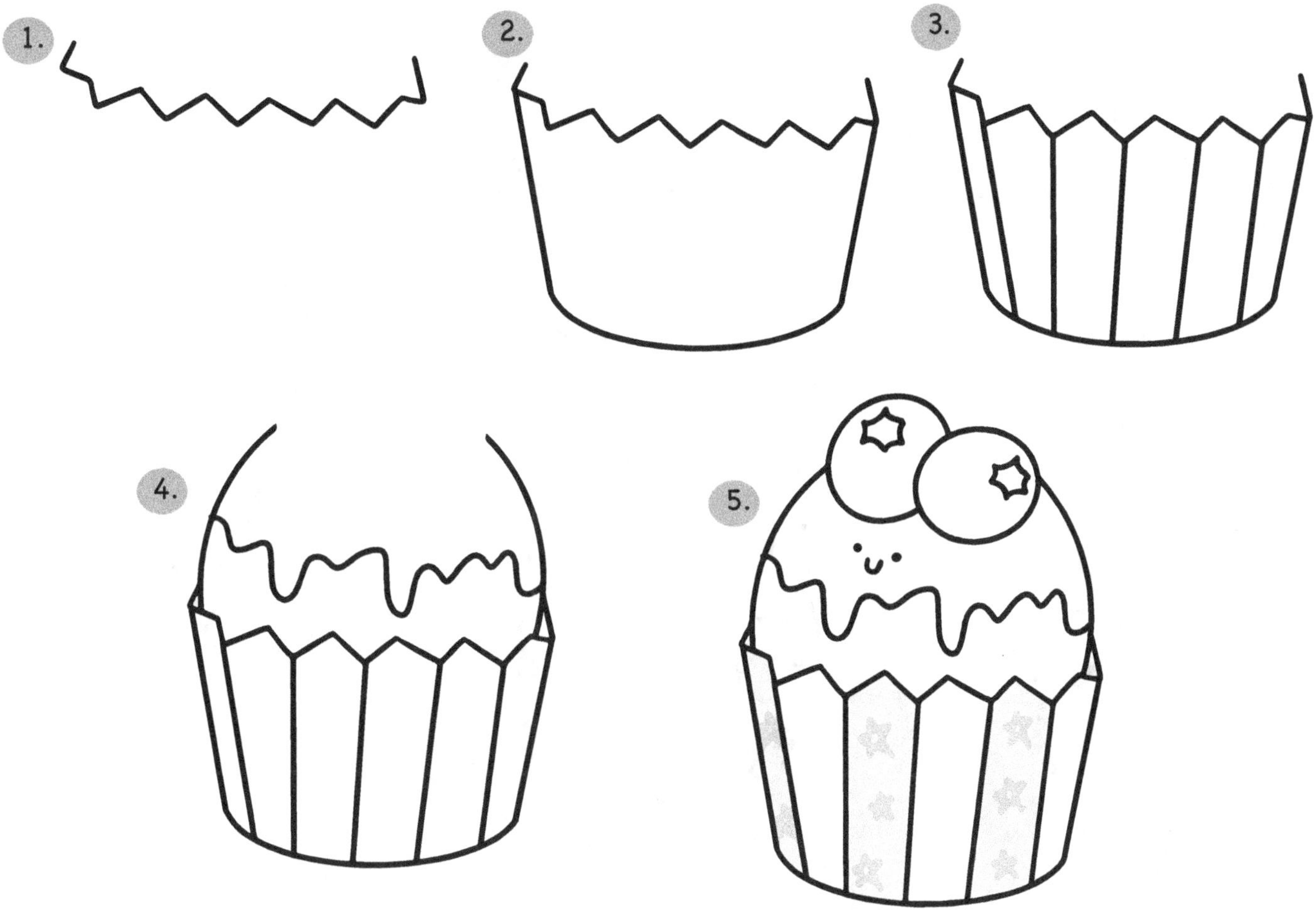

1.

2.

3.

4.

5.

Practice for drawing here.

Ice Cream

1.

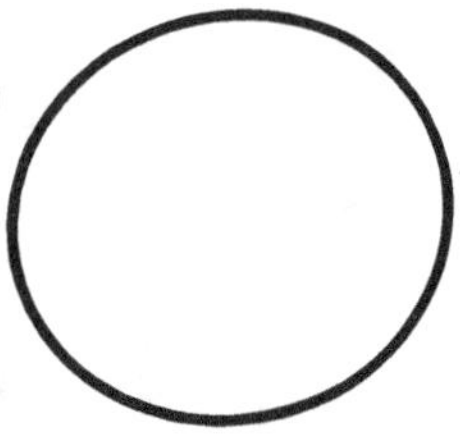

2.

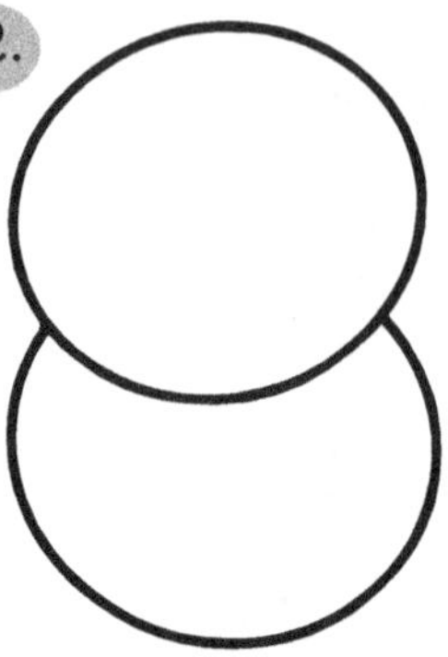

3.

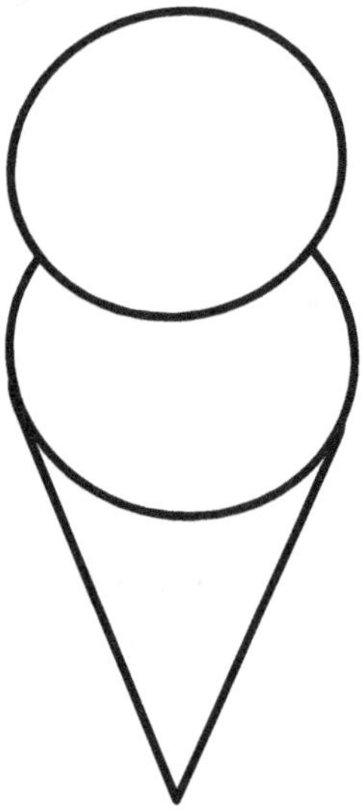

4.

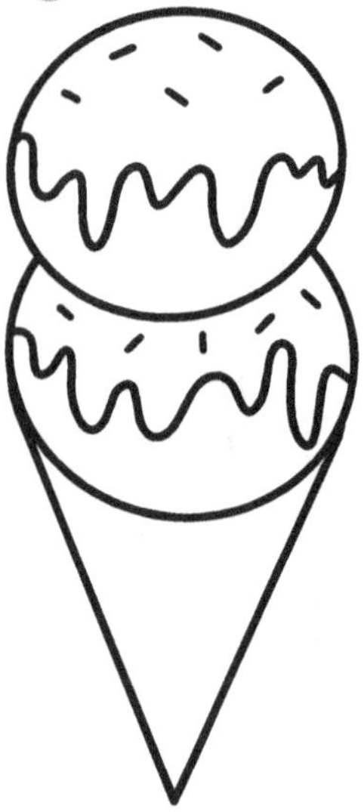

5.

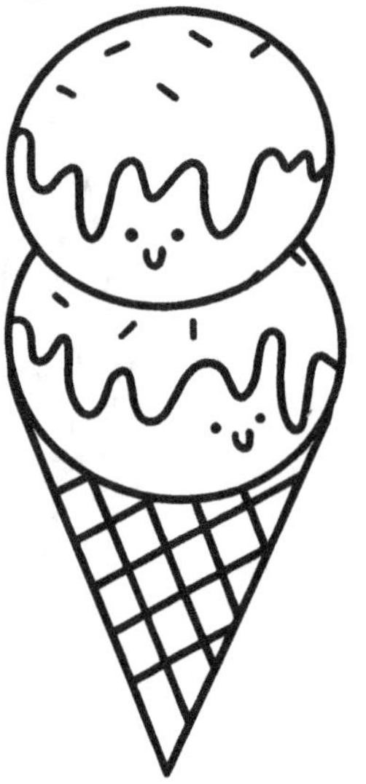

Practice for drawing here.

Donut

1. 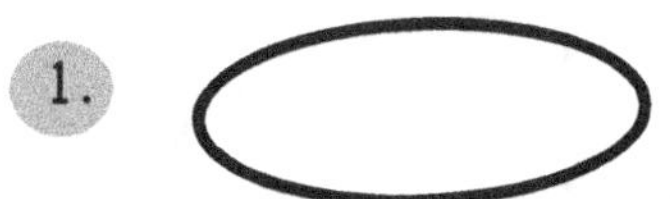

2. 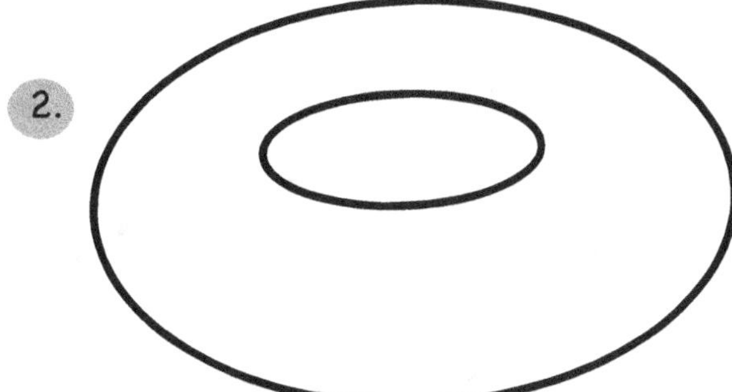

3. 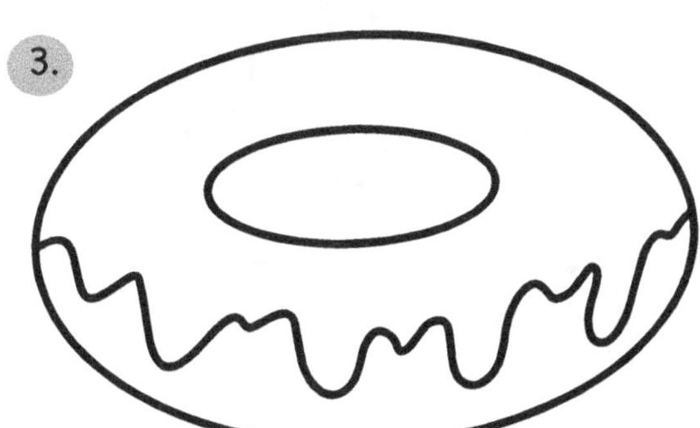

4. 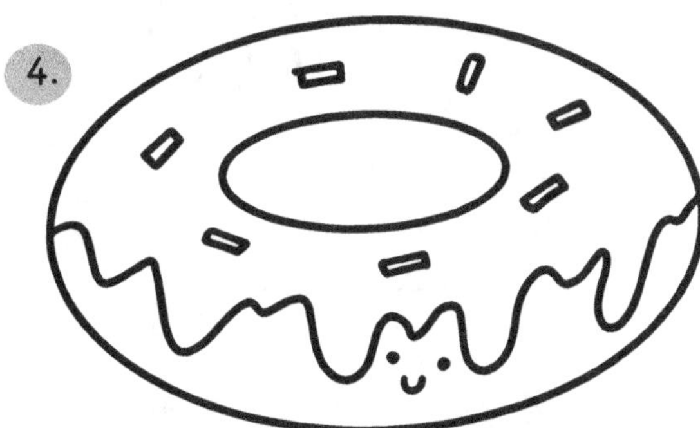

Practice for drawing here.

Omurice

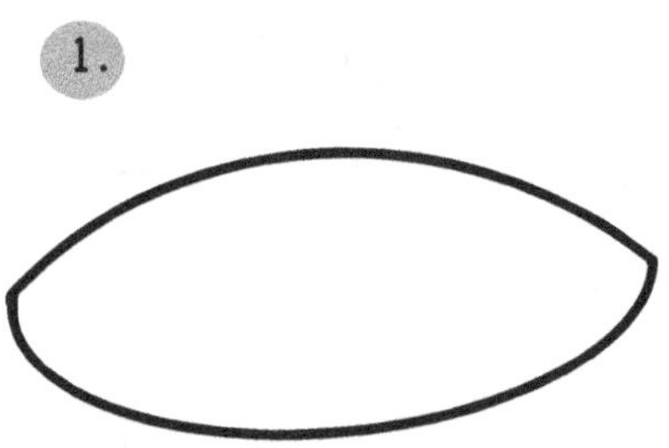 1.

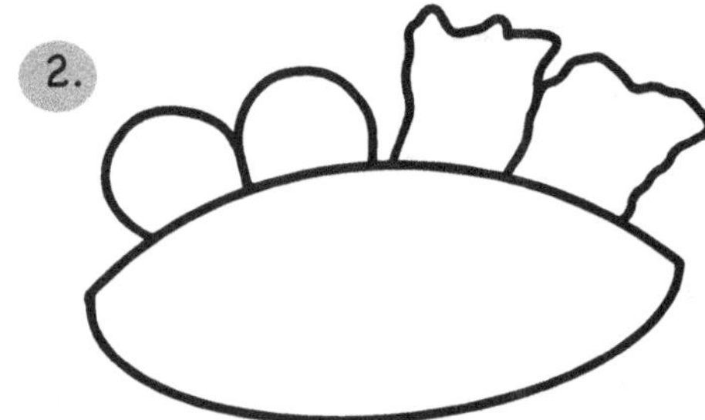 2.

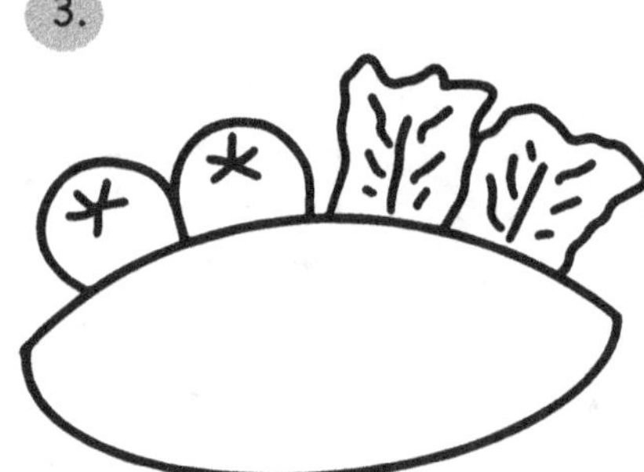 3.

 4.

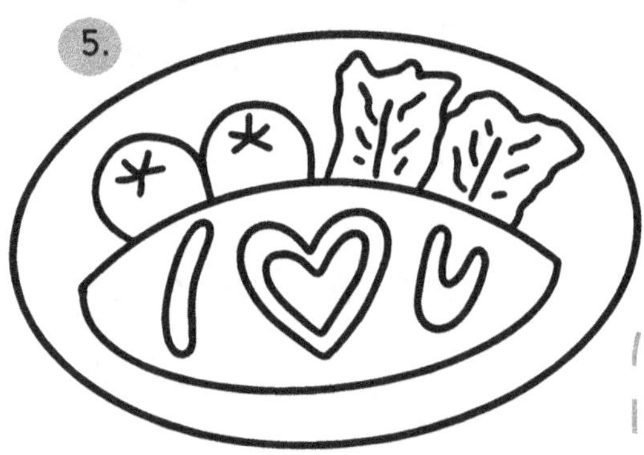 5.

Practice for drawing here.

Pizza

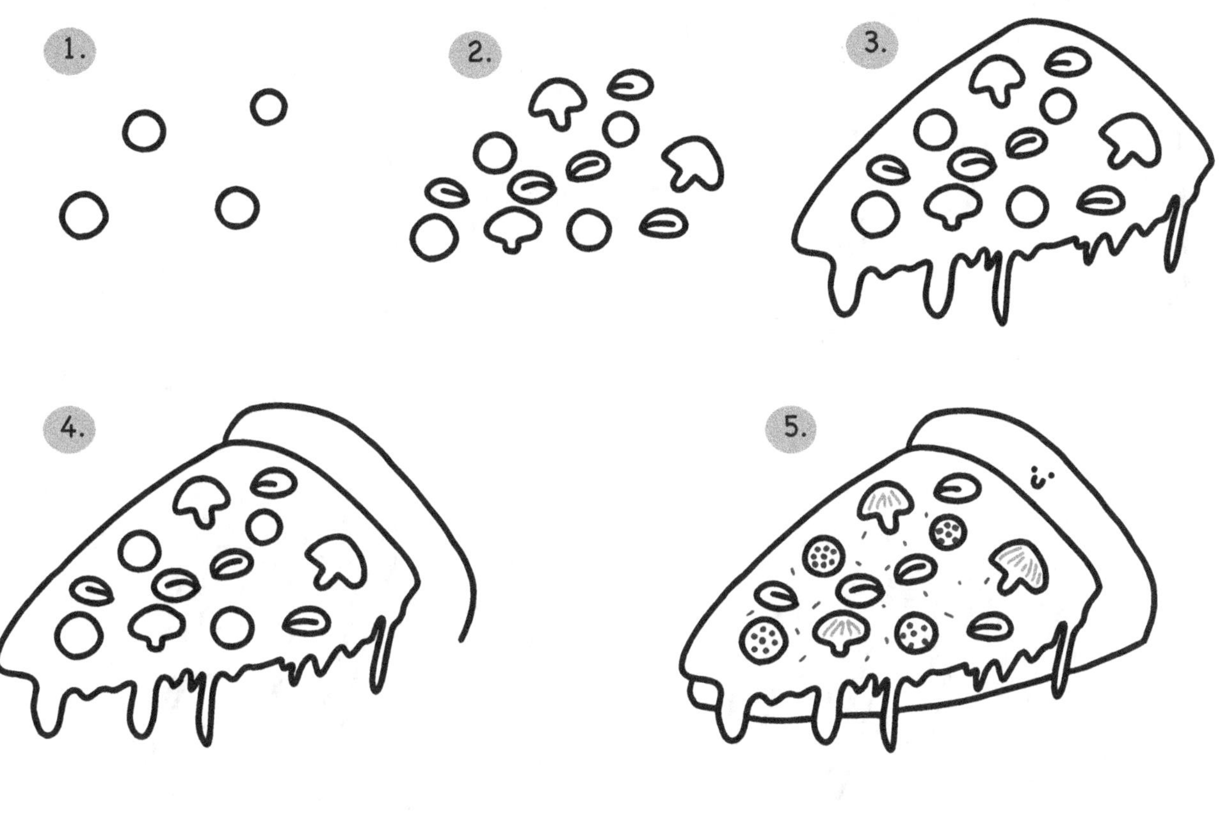

Practice for drawing here.

Fruit Sandwich

1.

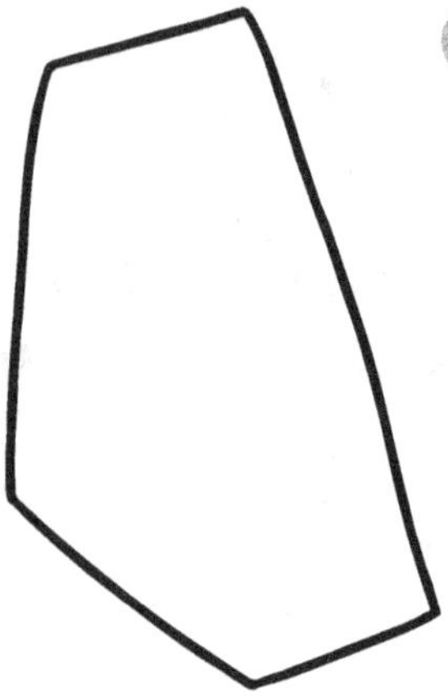

2.

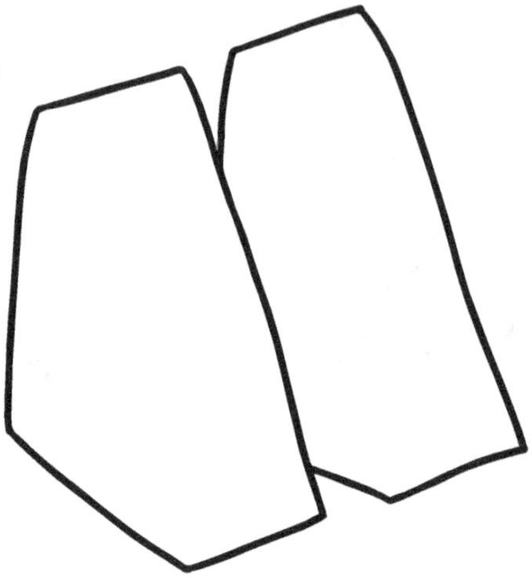

3.

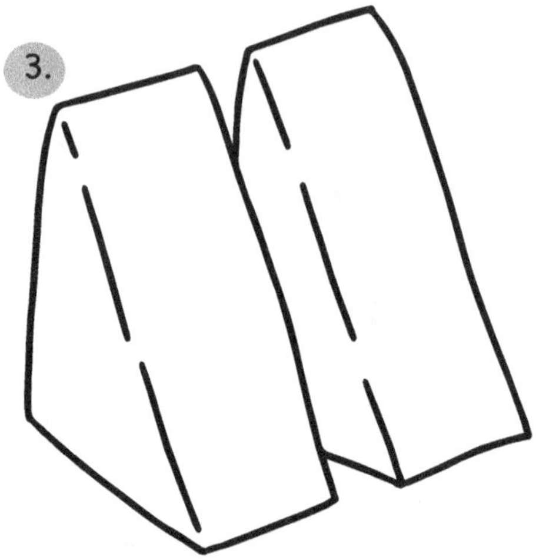

4.

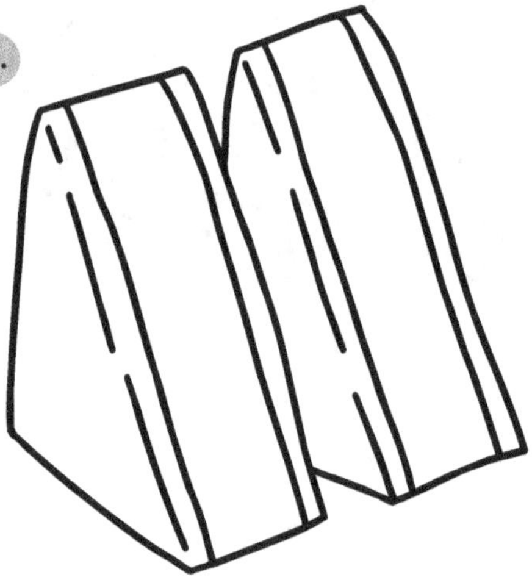

5.

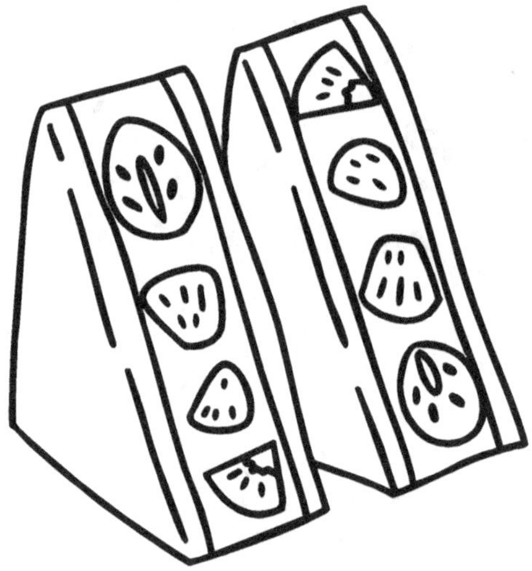

Practice for drawing here.

Orange Juice

1.

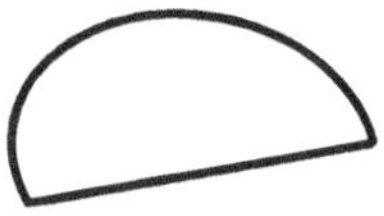

2.

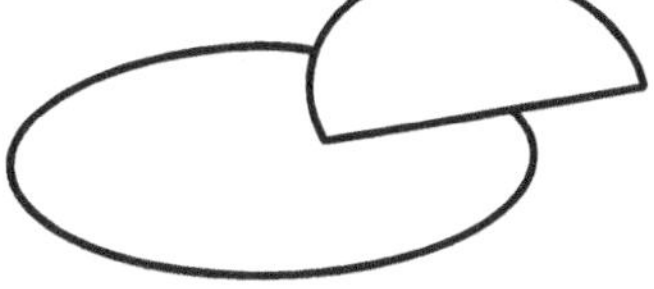

3.

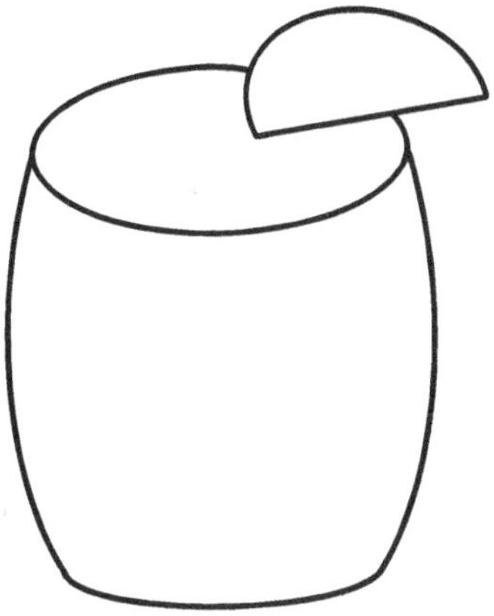

4.

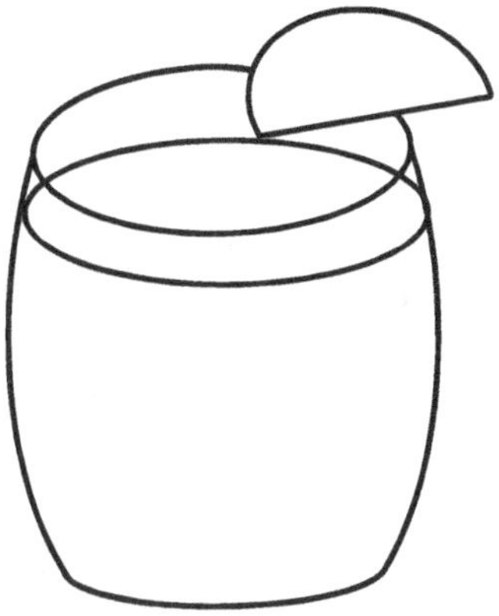

5.

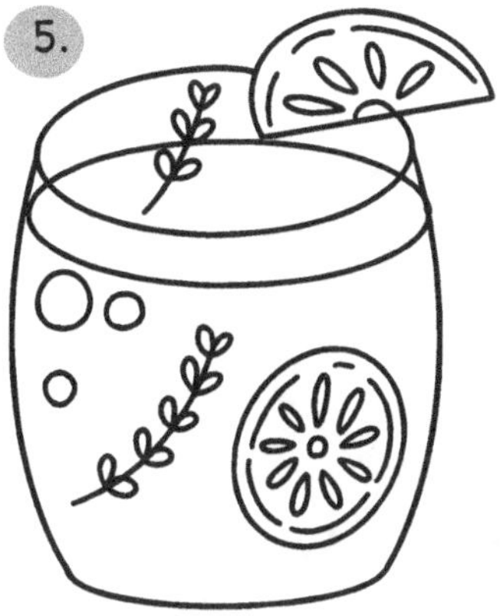

Practice for drawing here.

Wool scarf

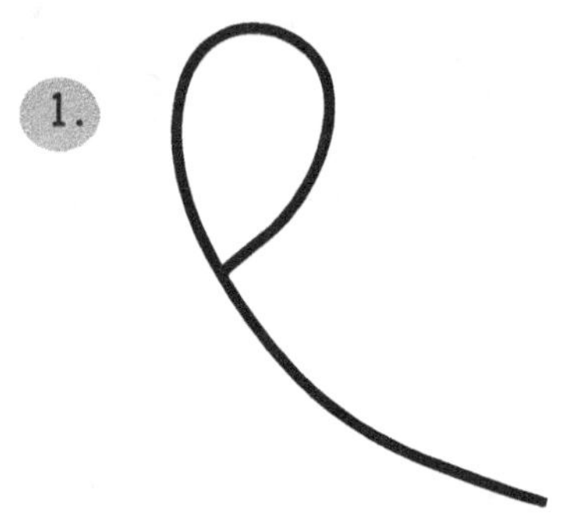 1.

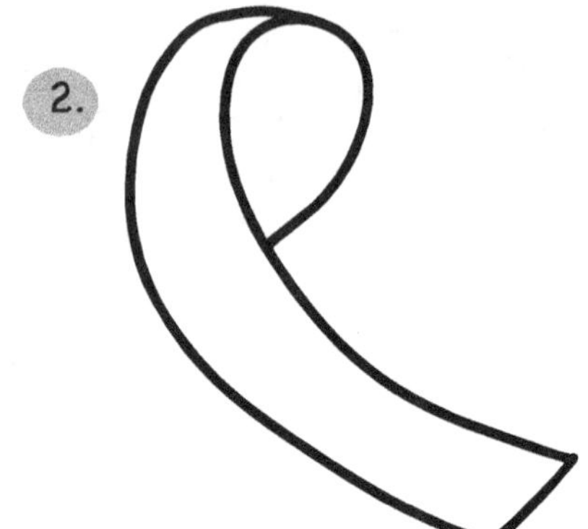 2.

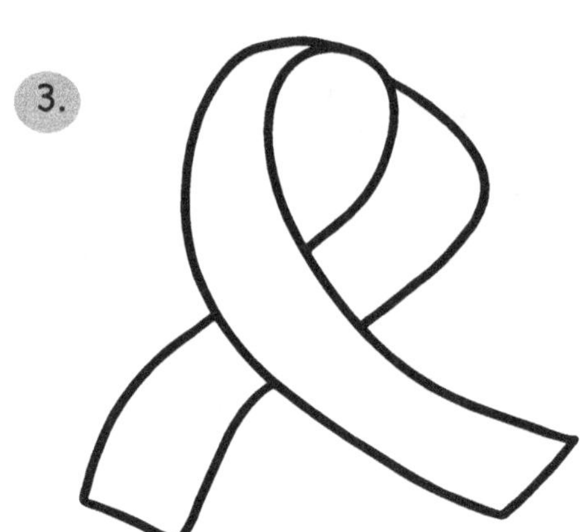 3.

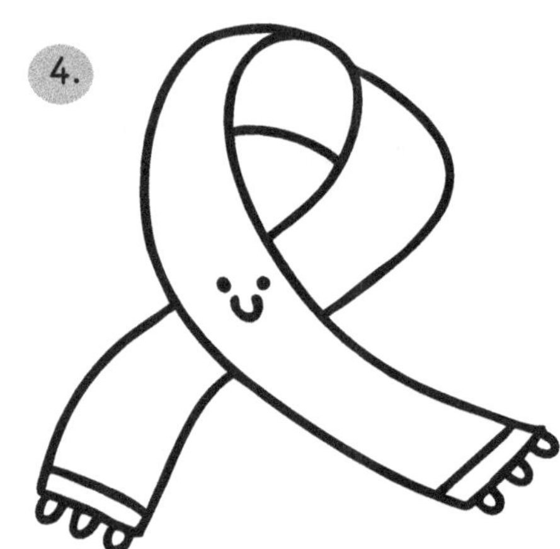 4.

Practice for drawing here.

Turtleneck sweater

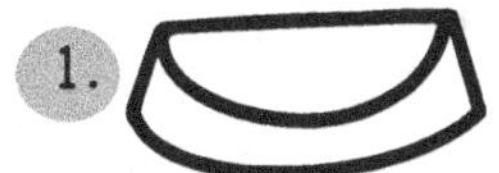

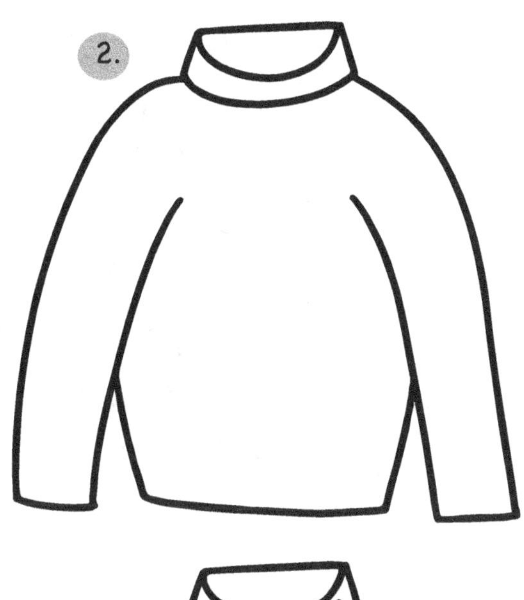

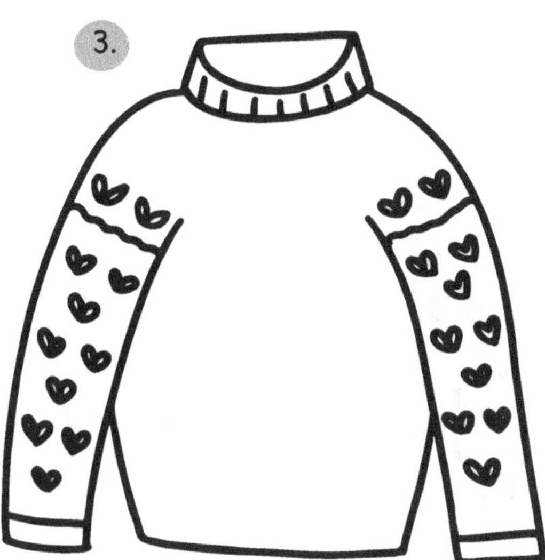

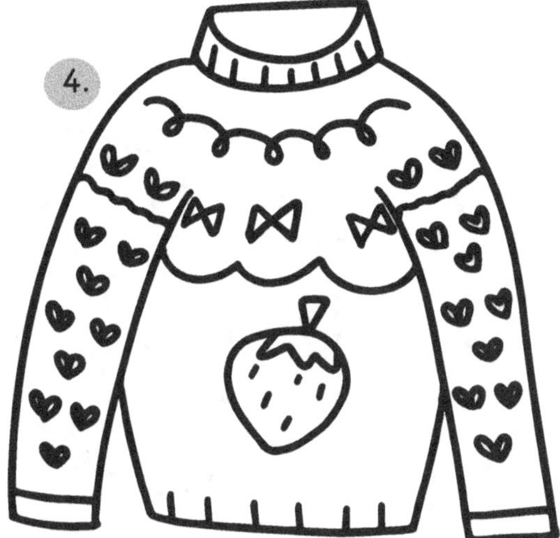

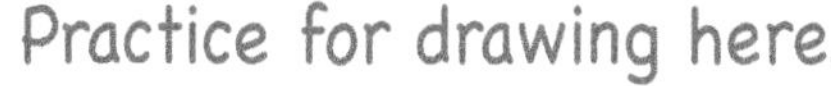

Practice for drawing here.

Sock

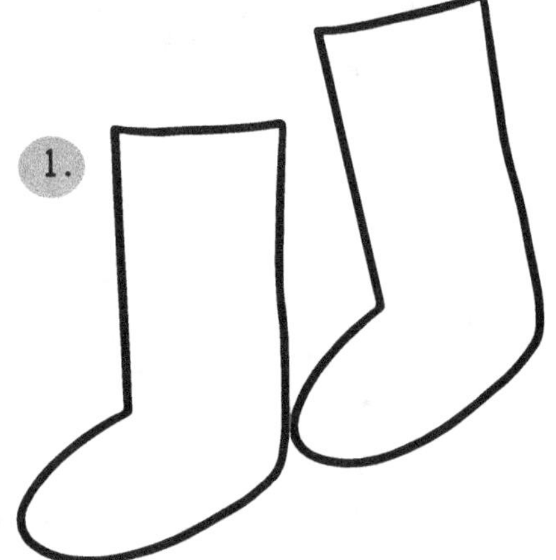 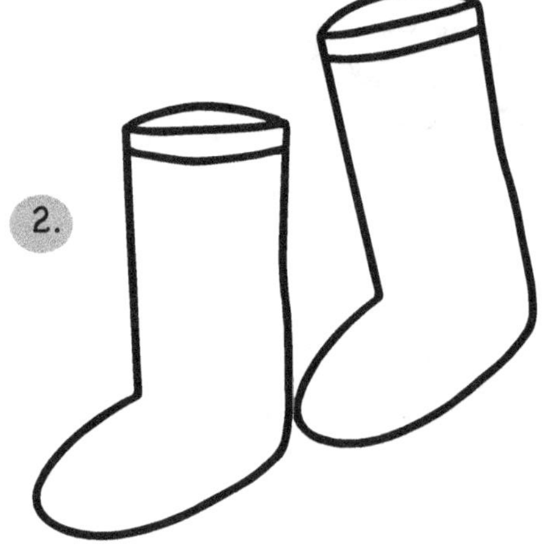

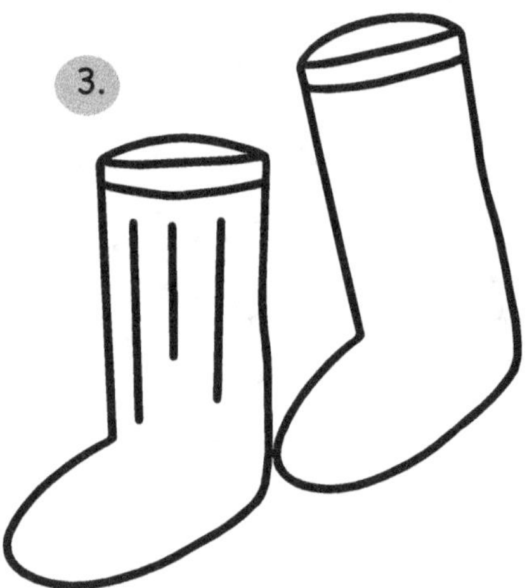 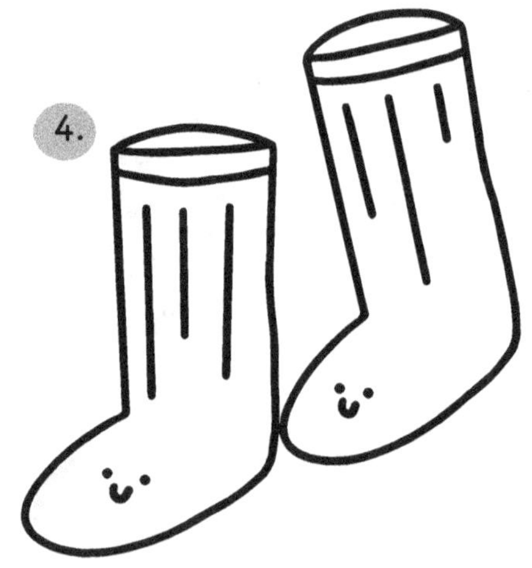

Practice for drawing here.

Pajamas

1.

2.

3.

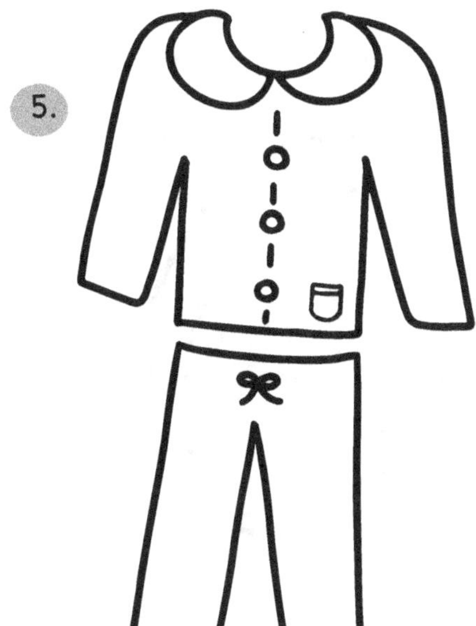

4.

5.

Practice for drawing here.

51.

Over-ear headphones

1.

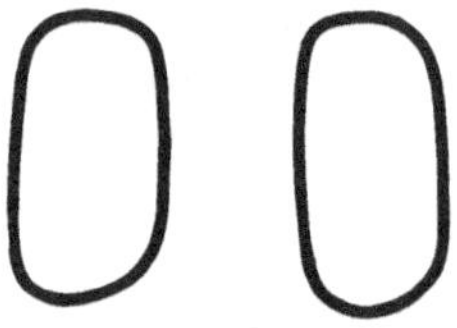

2.

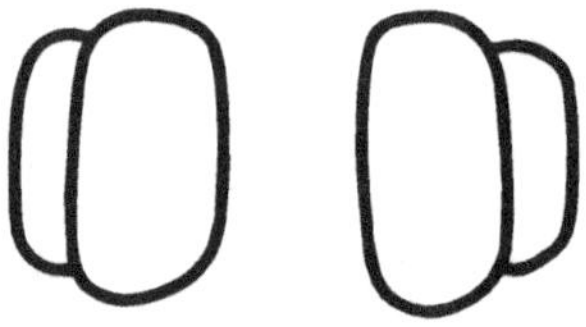

3.

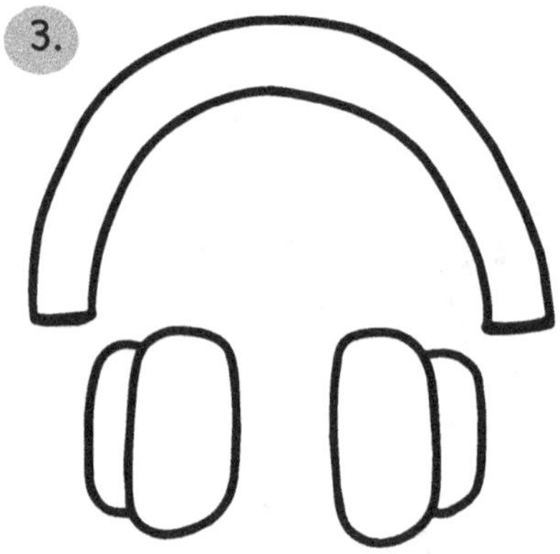

4.

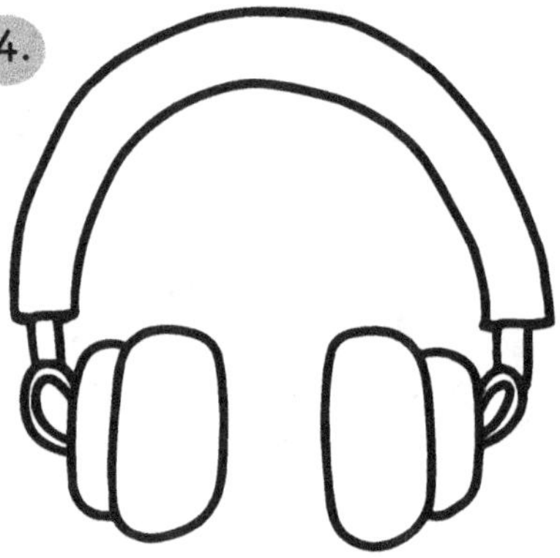

Practice for drawing here.

Luggage

1.

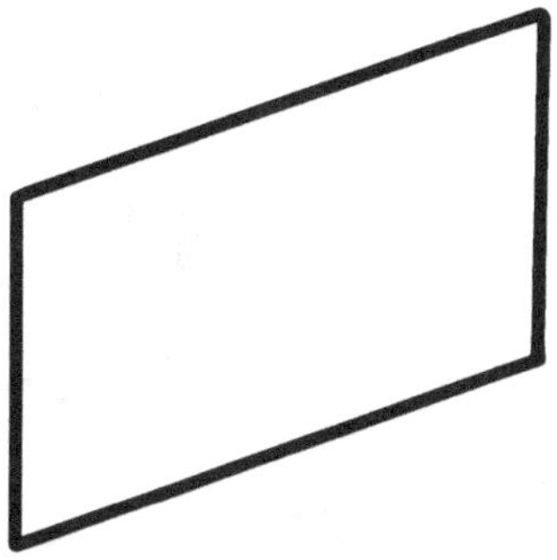

2.

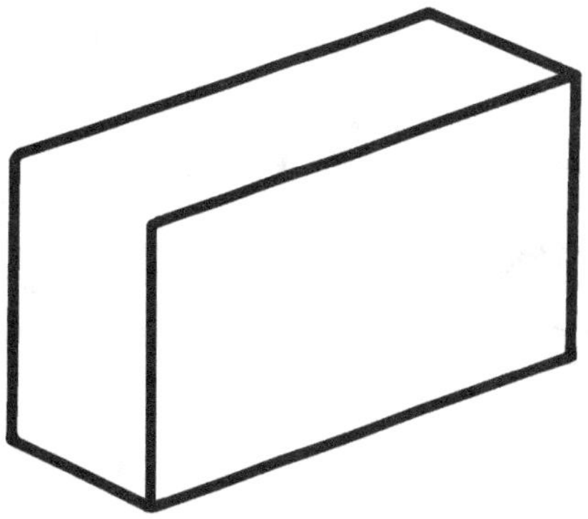

3.

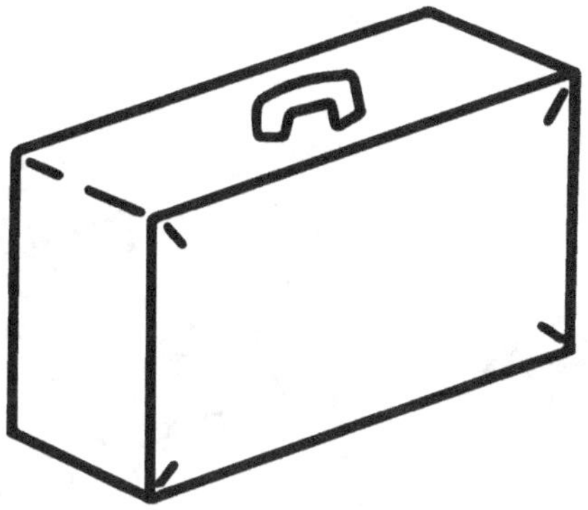

4.

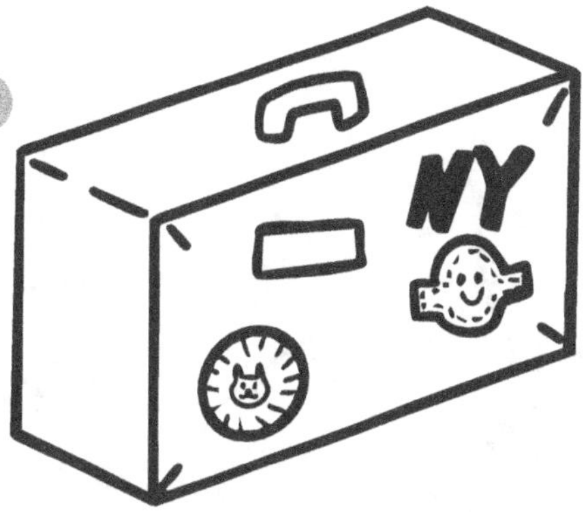

Practice for drawing here.

Canvas shoes

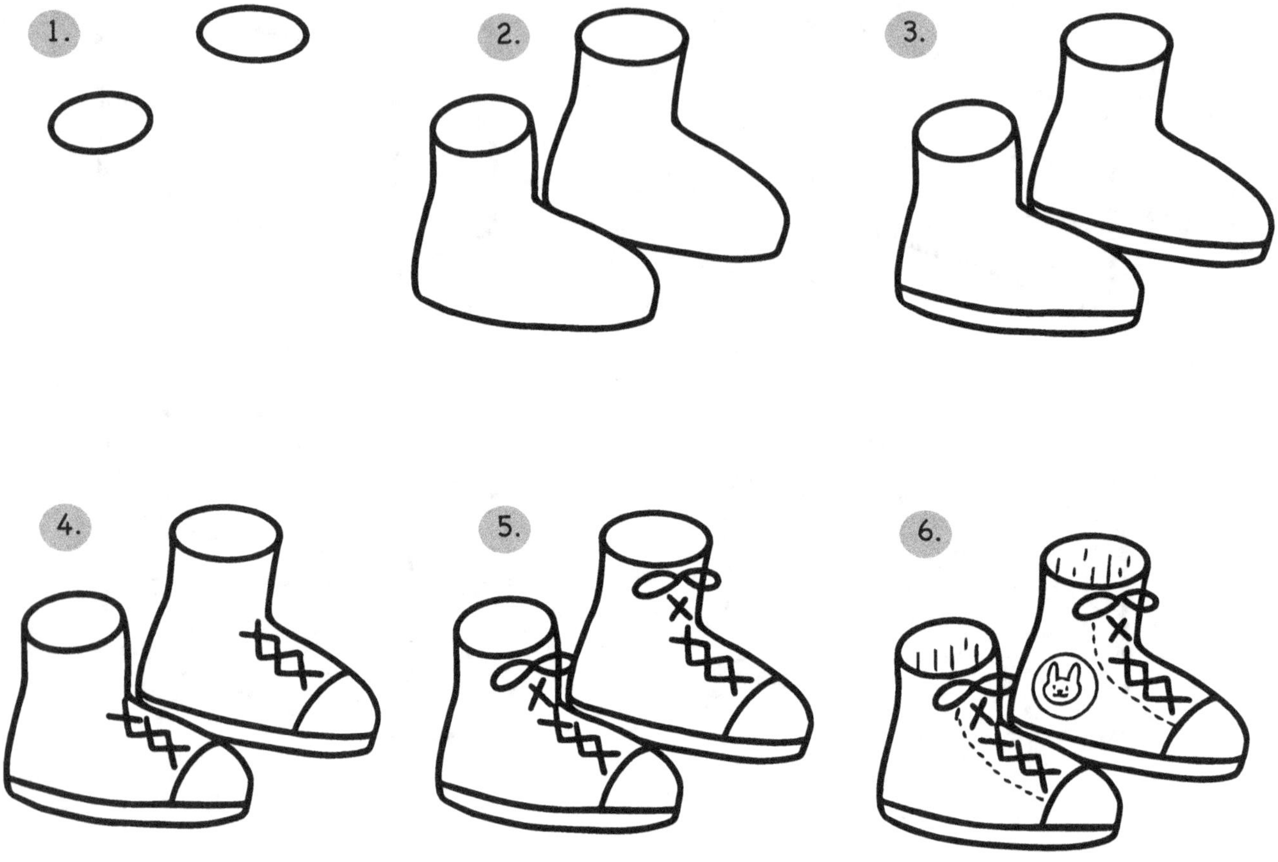

1.
2.
3.
4.
5.
6.

Practice for drawing here.

Camera

 1. 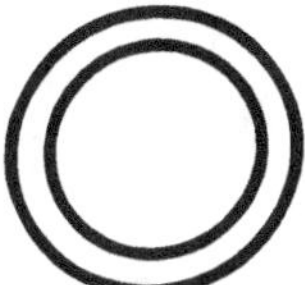

2. 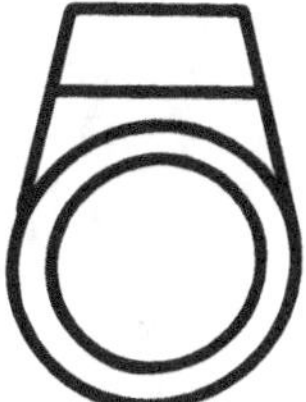

3. 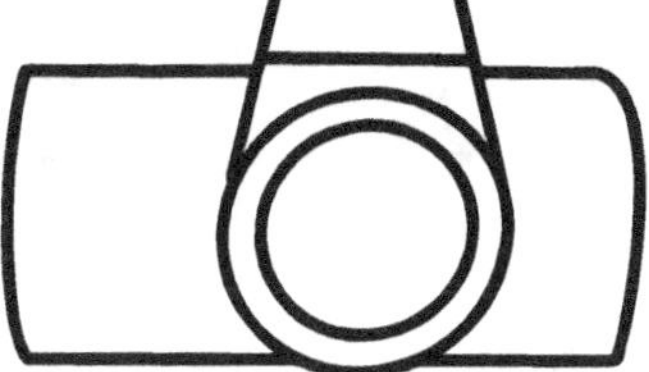

4. 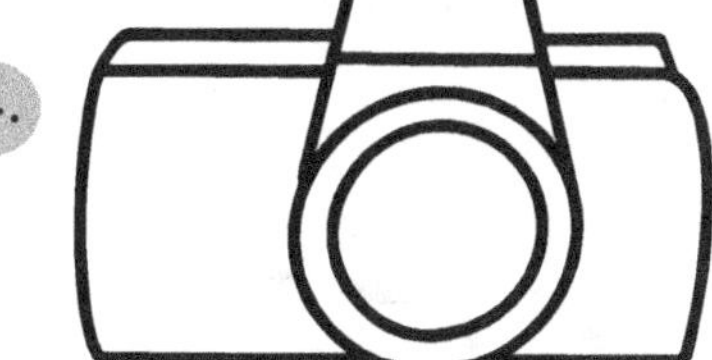

5. 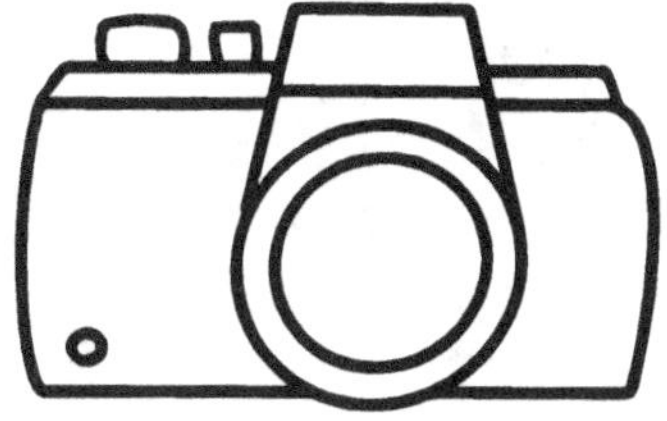

6. 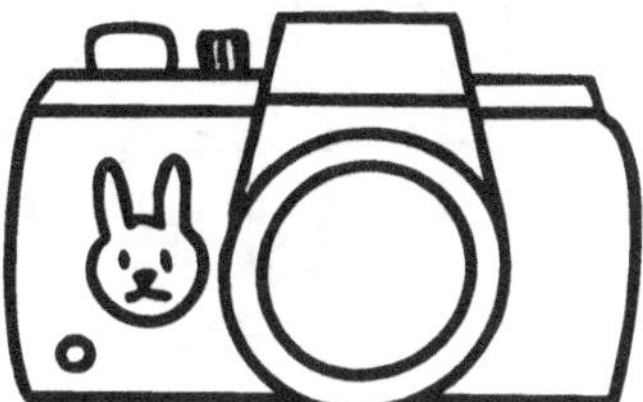

Practice for drawing here.

Backpack

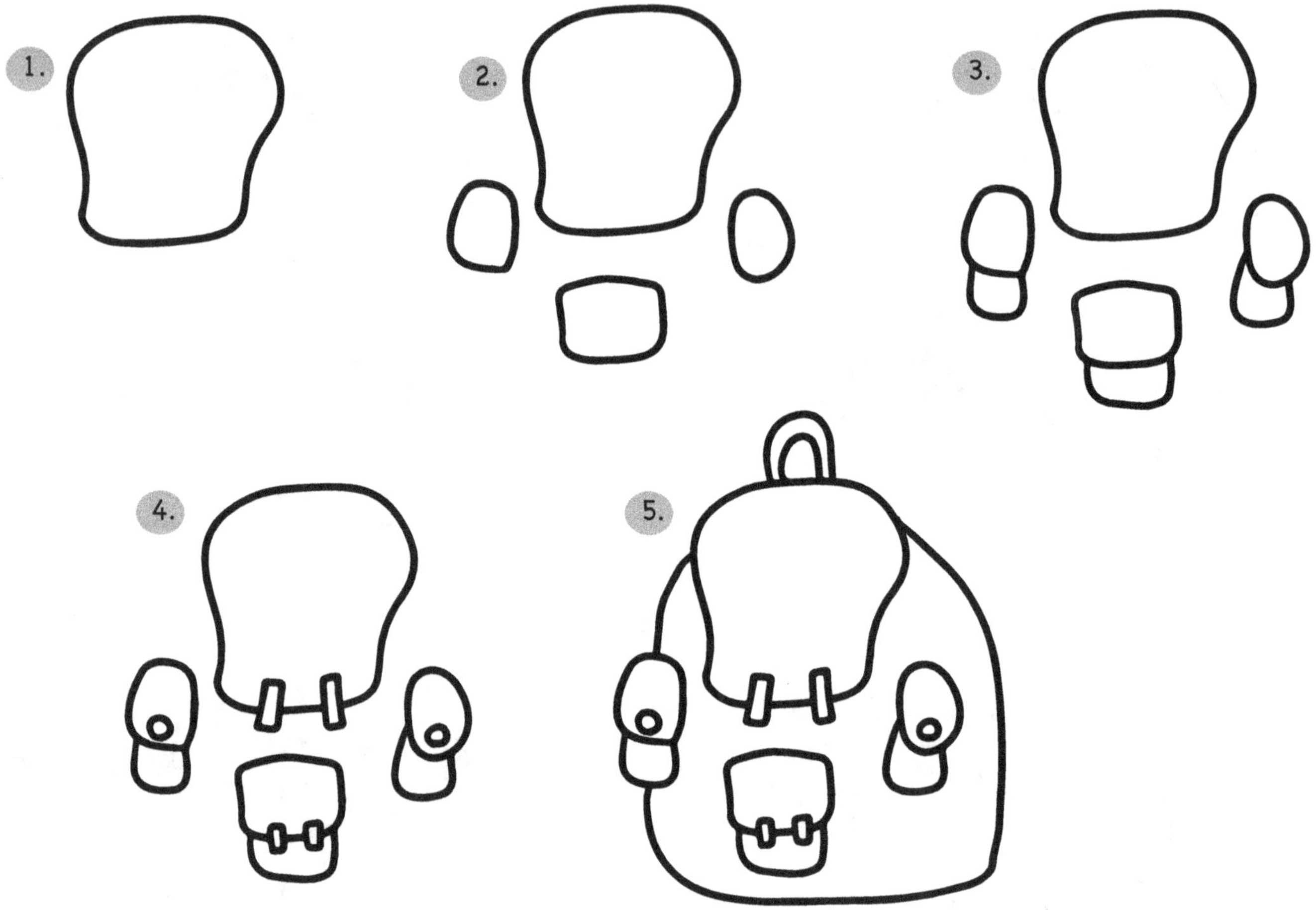

1.

2.

3.

4.

5.

Practice for drawing here.

Binoculars

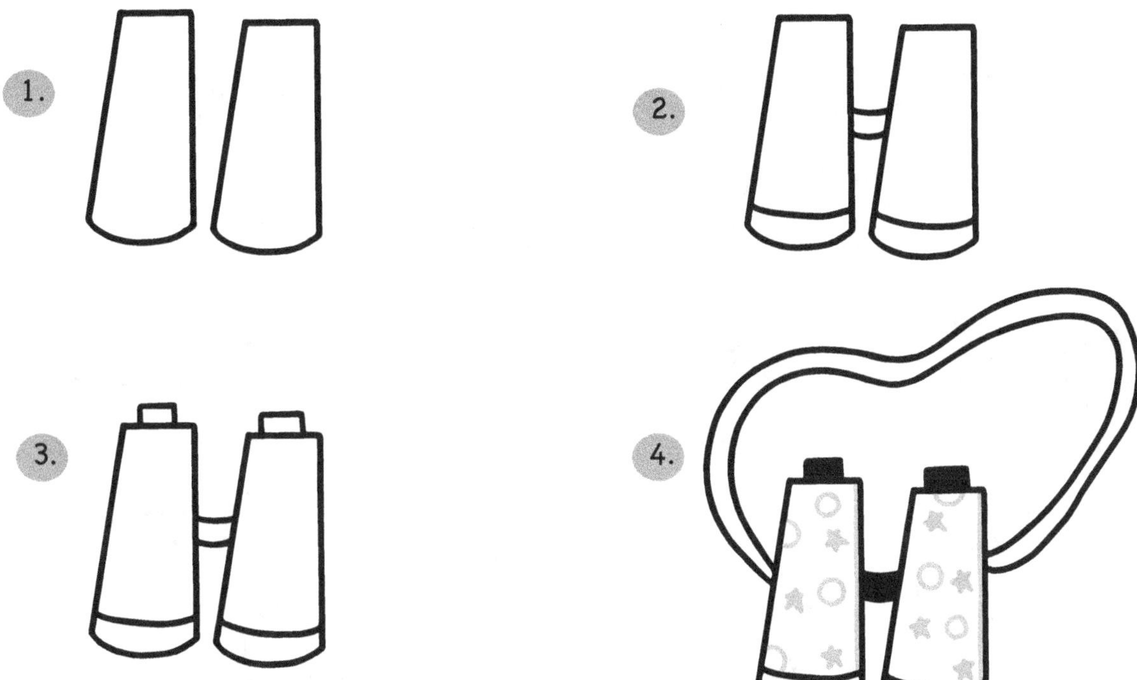

Practice for drawing here.

Cactus

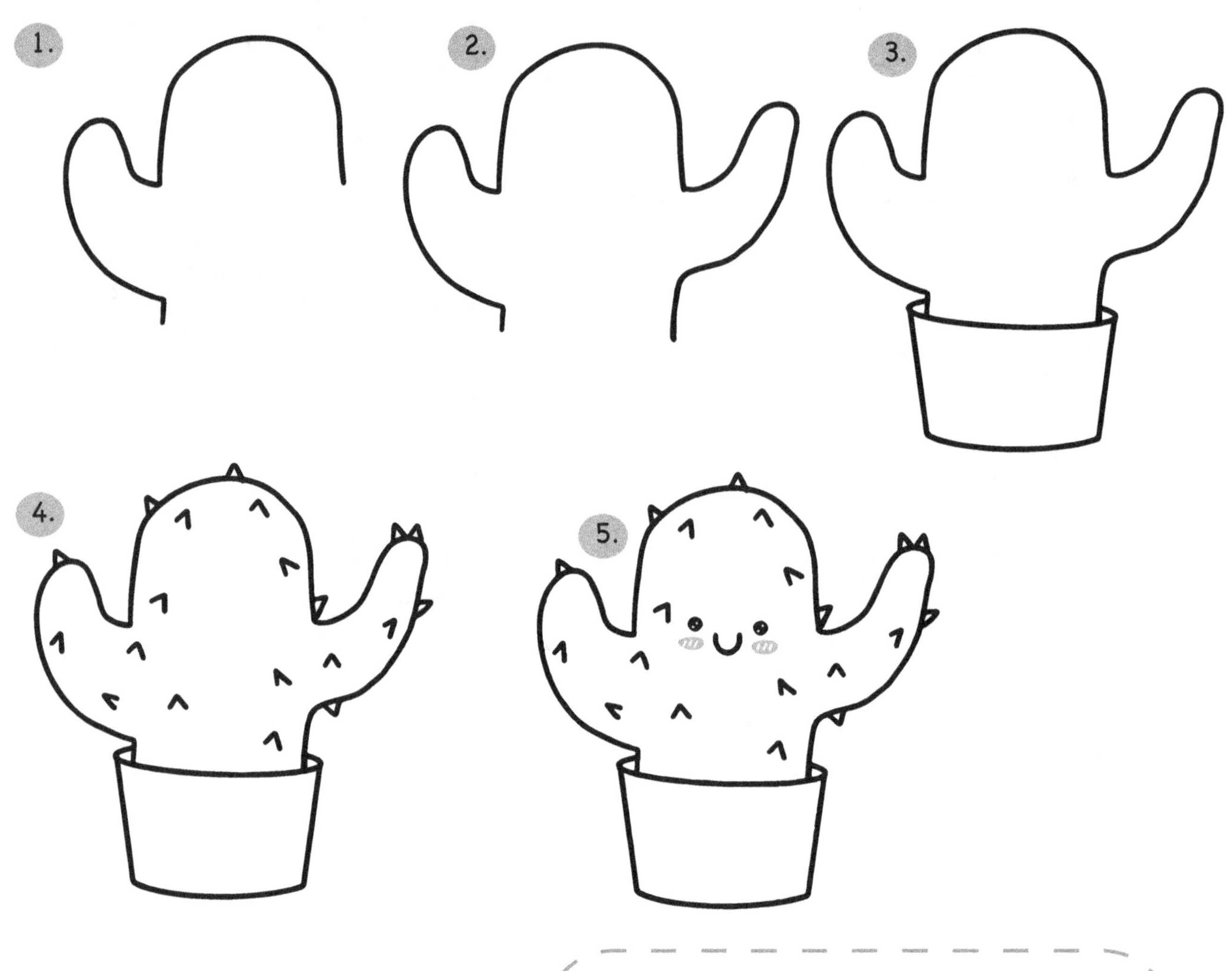

Practice for drawing here.

Flower vase

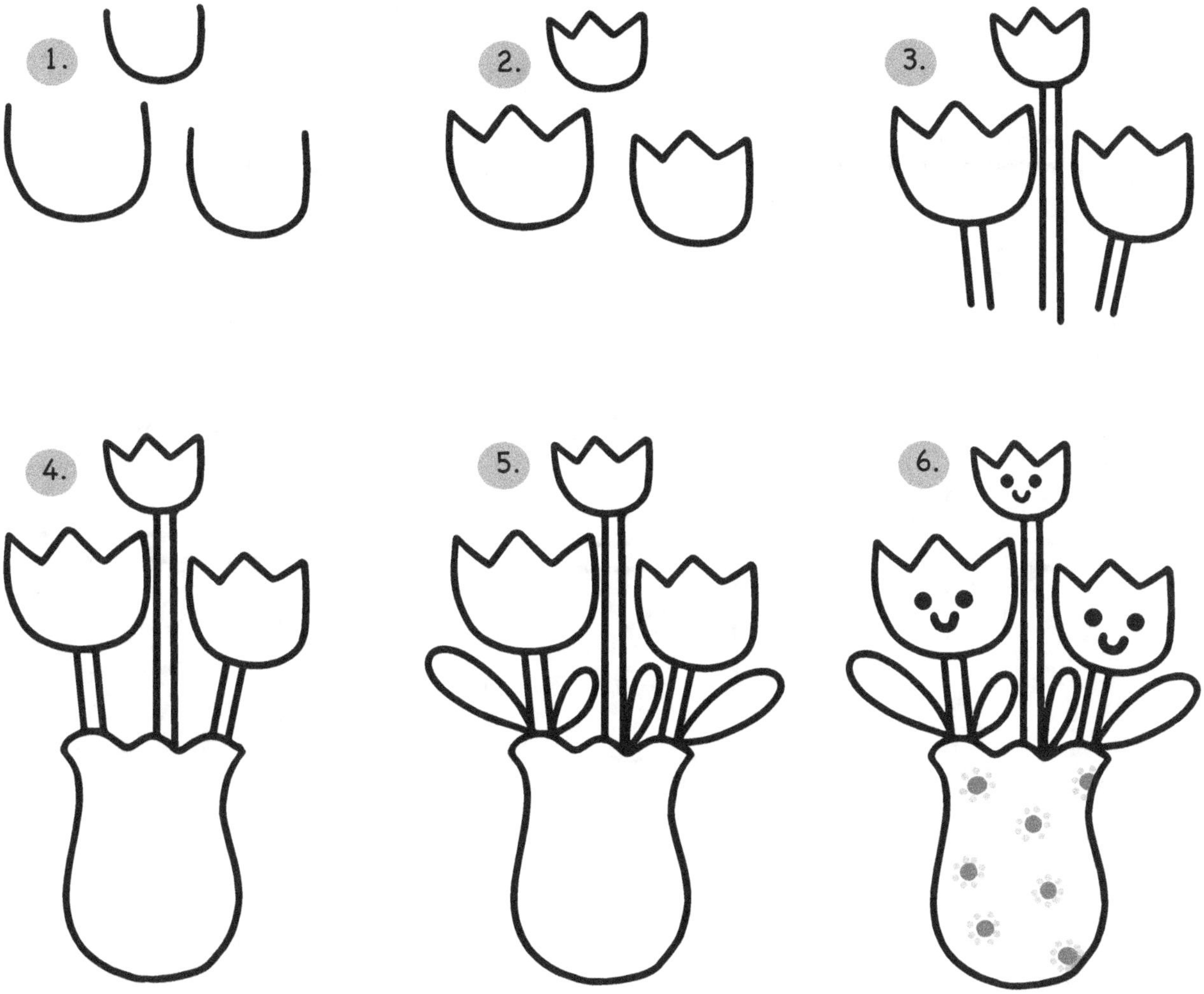

1.

2.

3.

4.

5.

6.

Practice for drawing here.

Jar

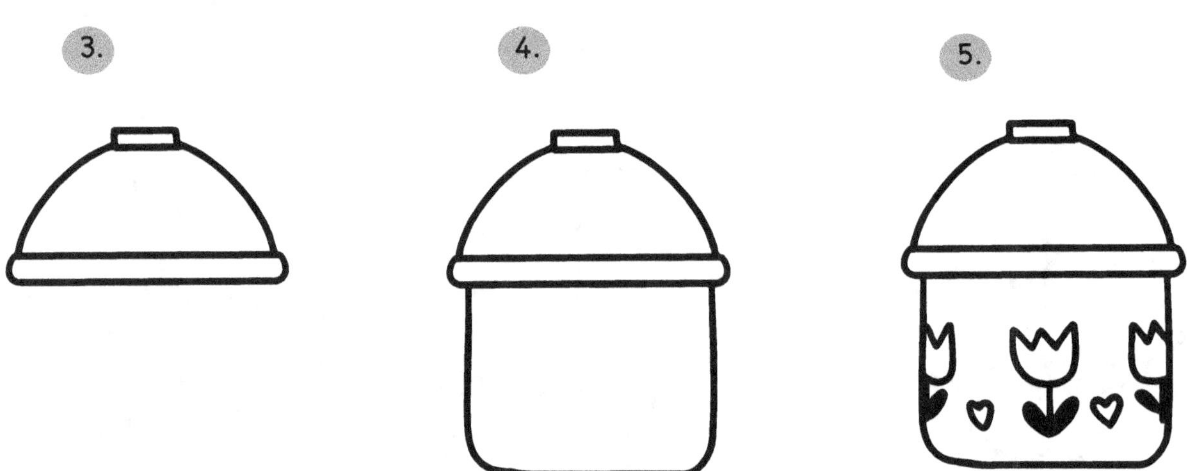

Practice for drawing here.

Coffee cup

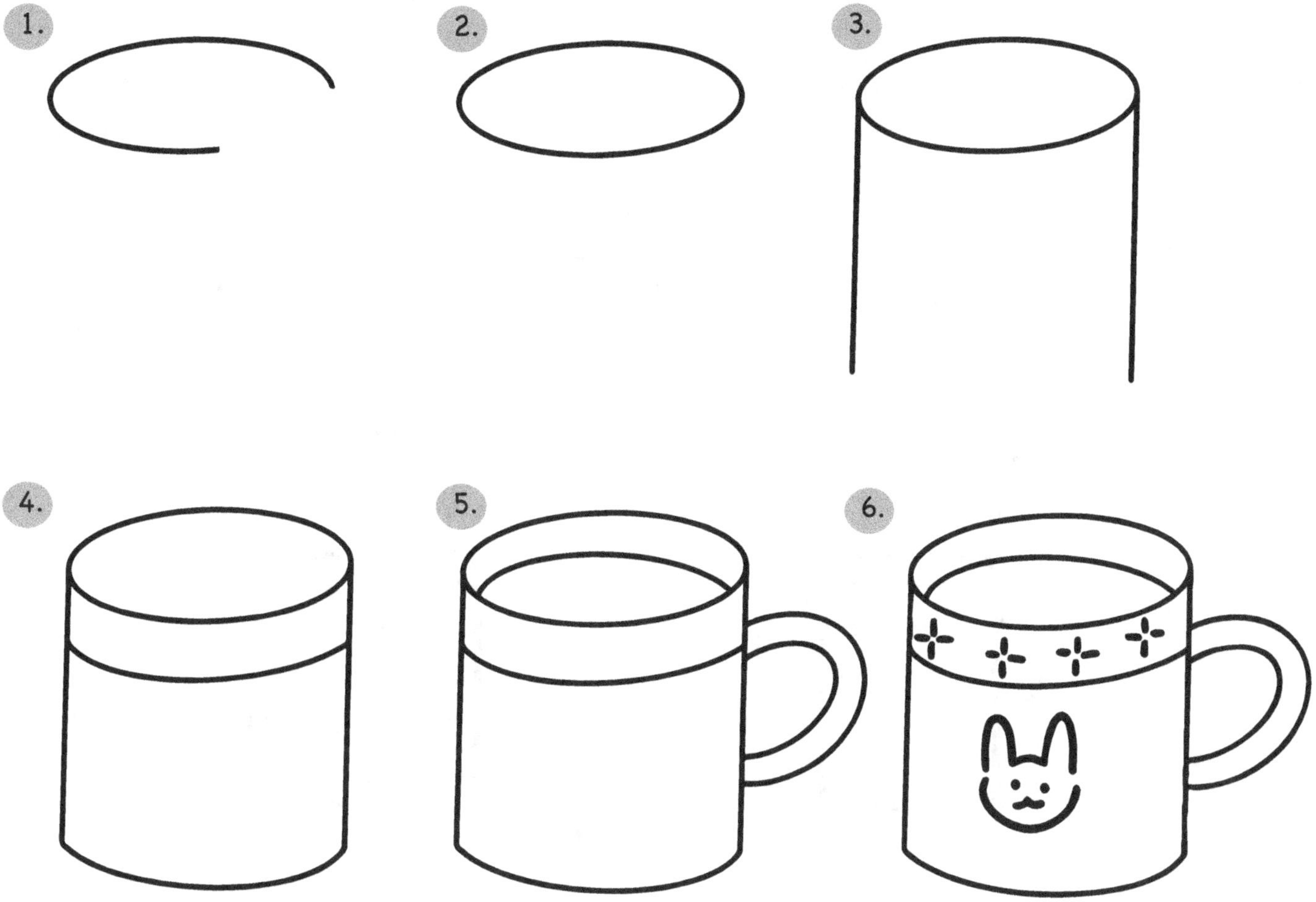

1.

2.

3.

4.

5.

6.

Practice for drawing here.

Cup Coffee filter

1.

2.

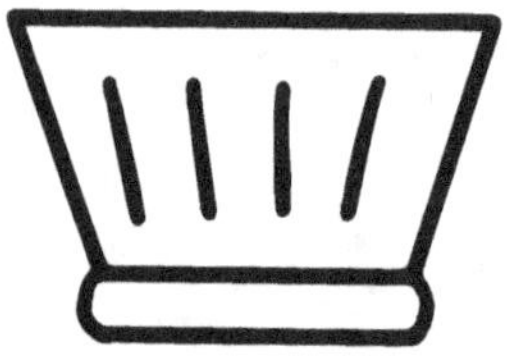

3.

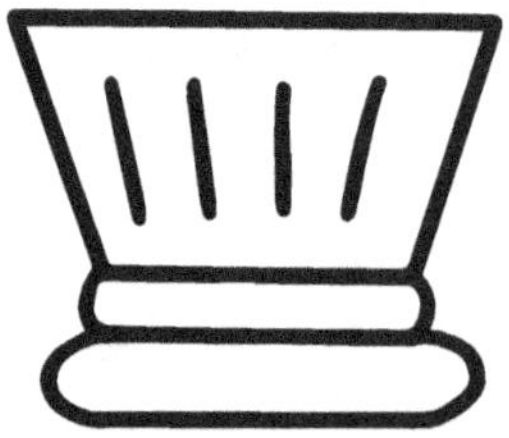

4.

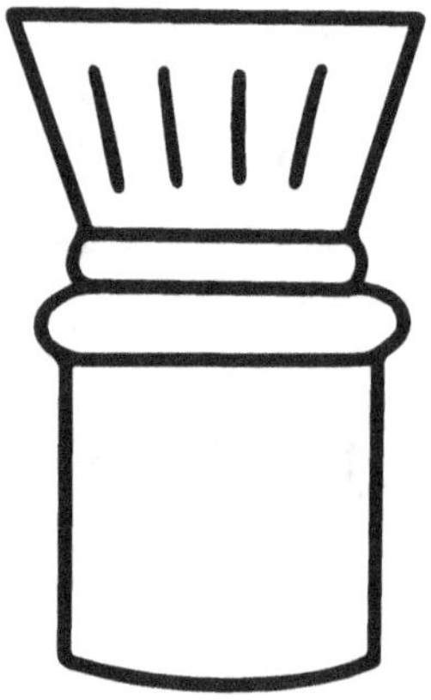

5.

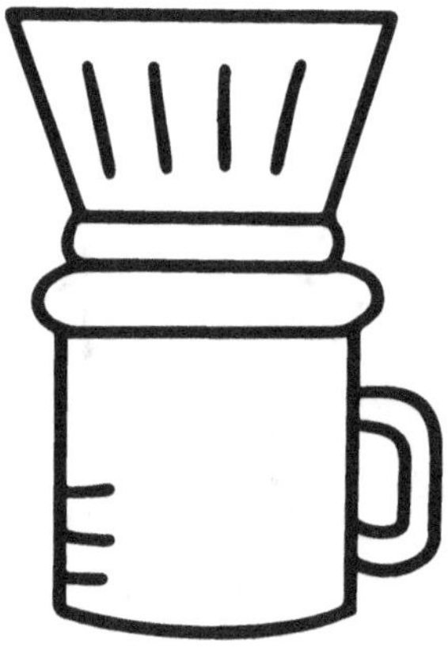

Practice for drawing here.

Laundry basket

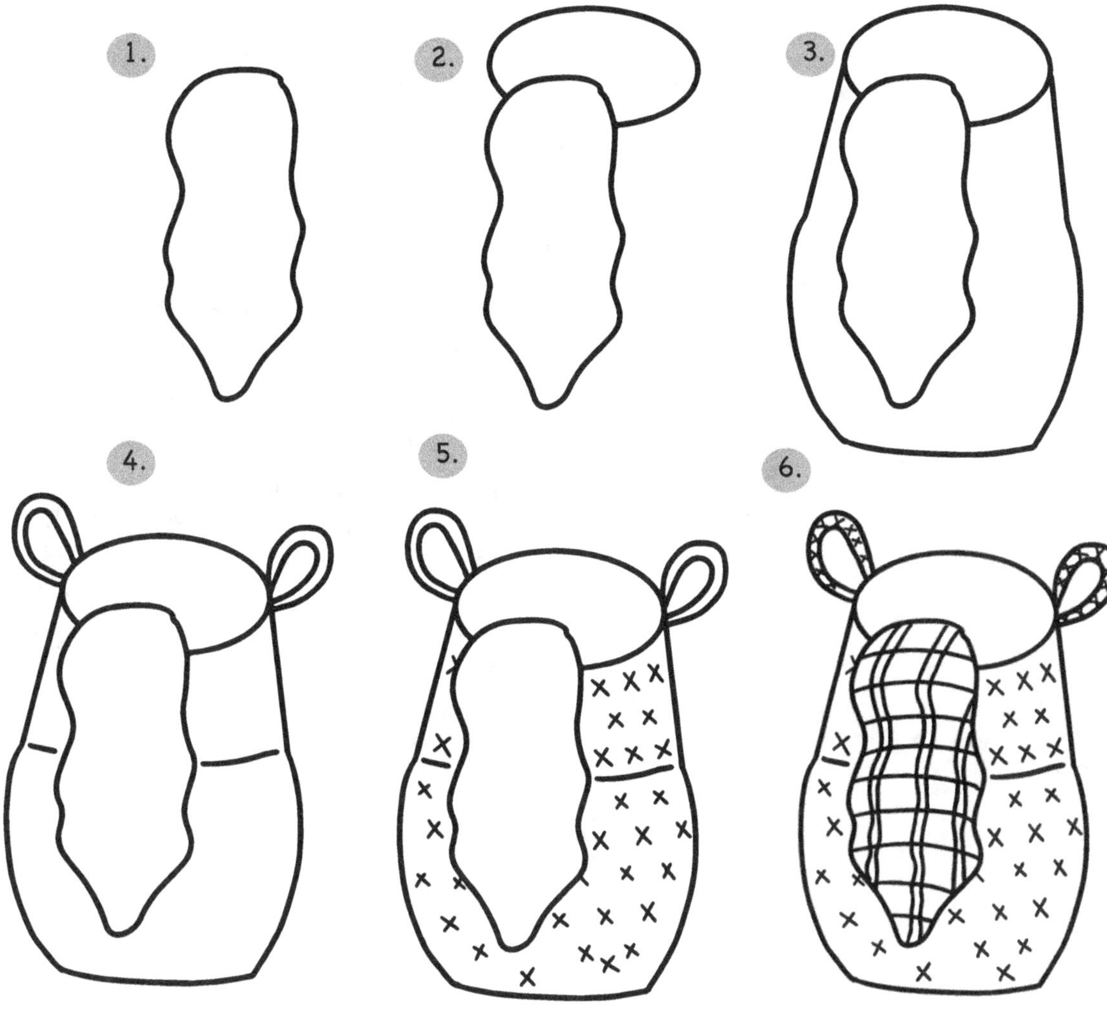

1.

2.

3.

4.

5.

6.

Practice for drawing here.

Notebook

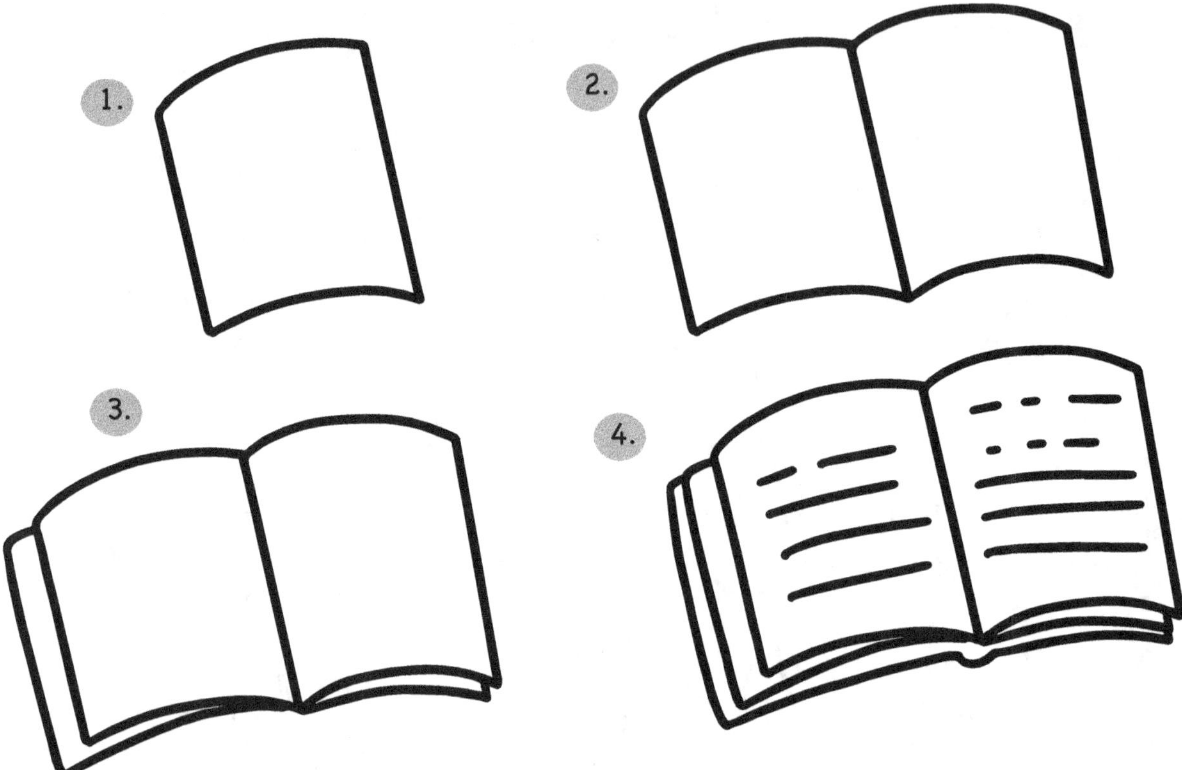

1.
2.
3.
4.

Practice for drawing here.

Pillow

1.

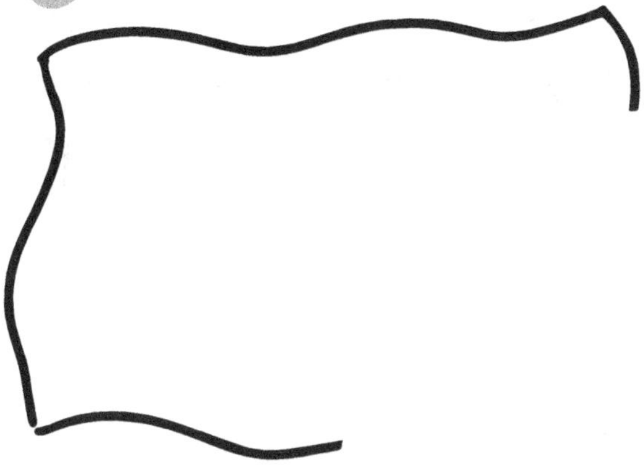

2.

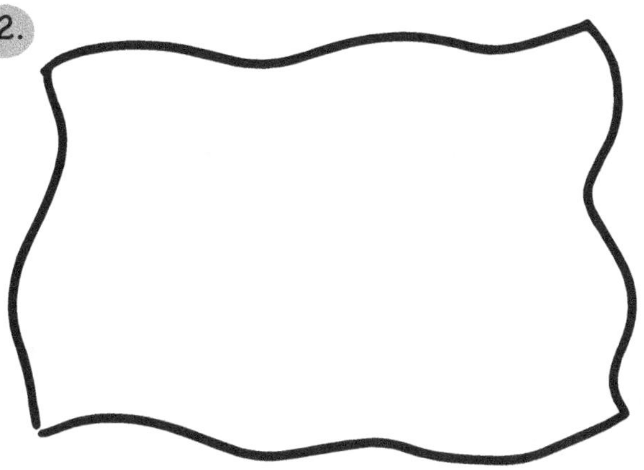

3.

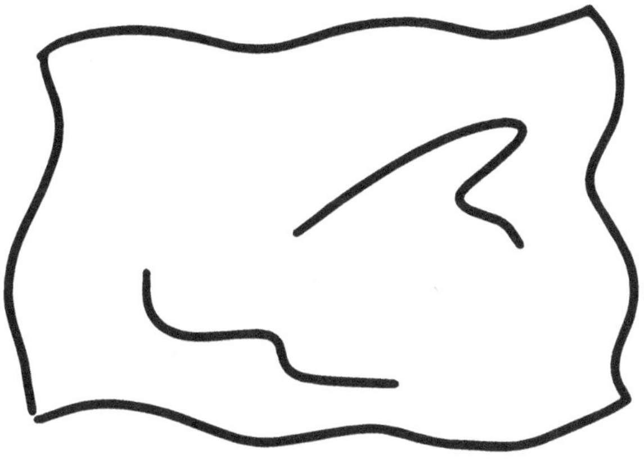

4.

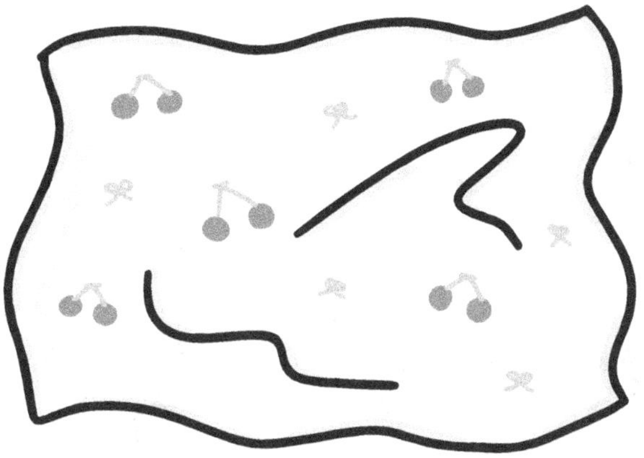

Practice for drawing here.

Sofa

1.

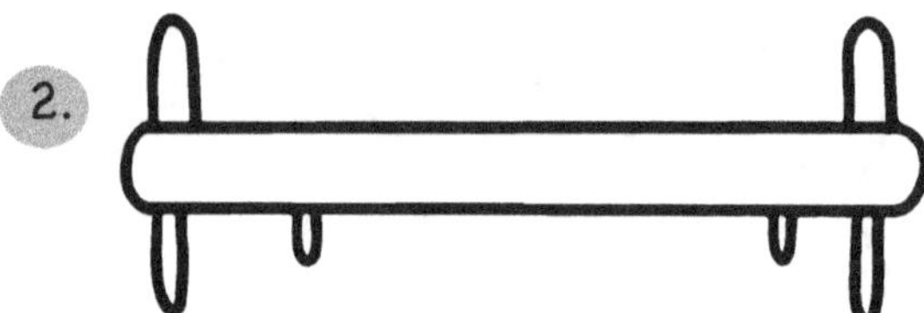

2.

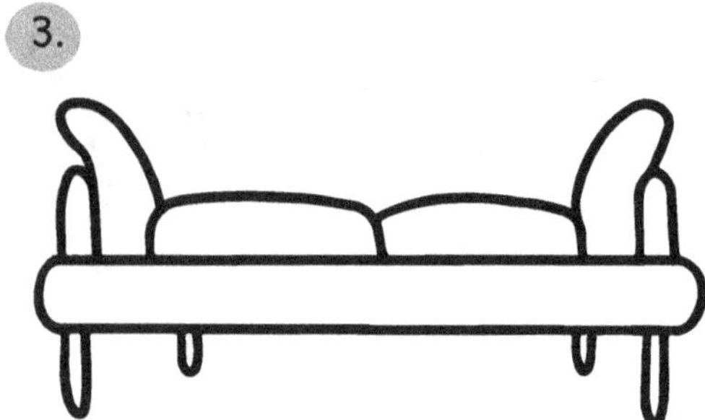

3.

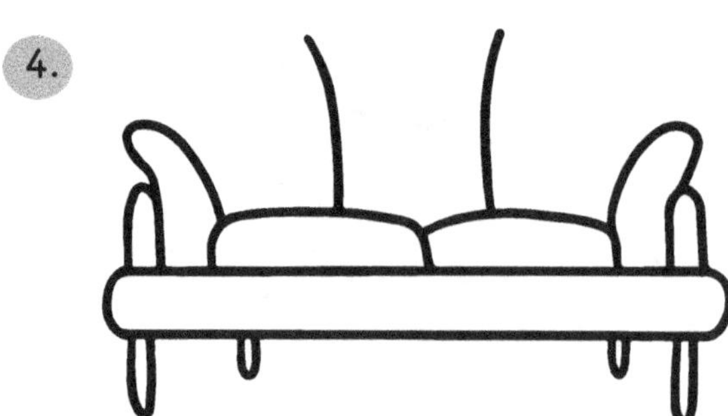

4.

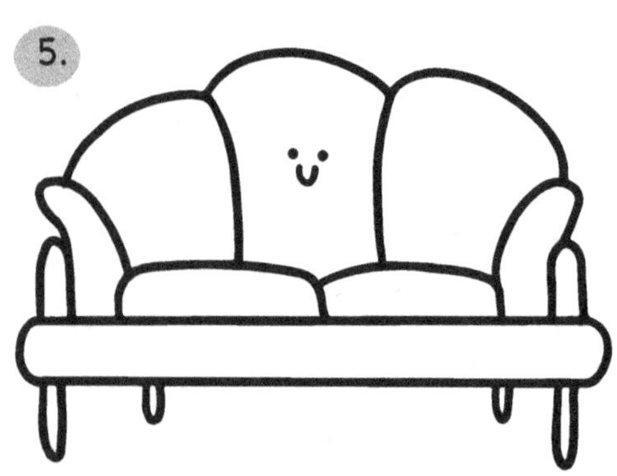

5.

Taper

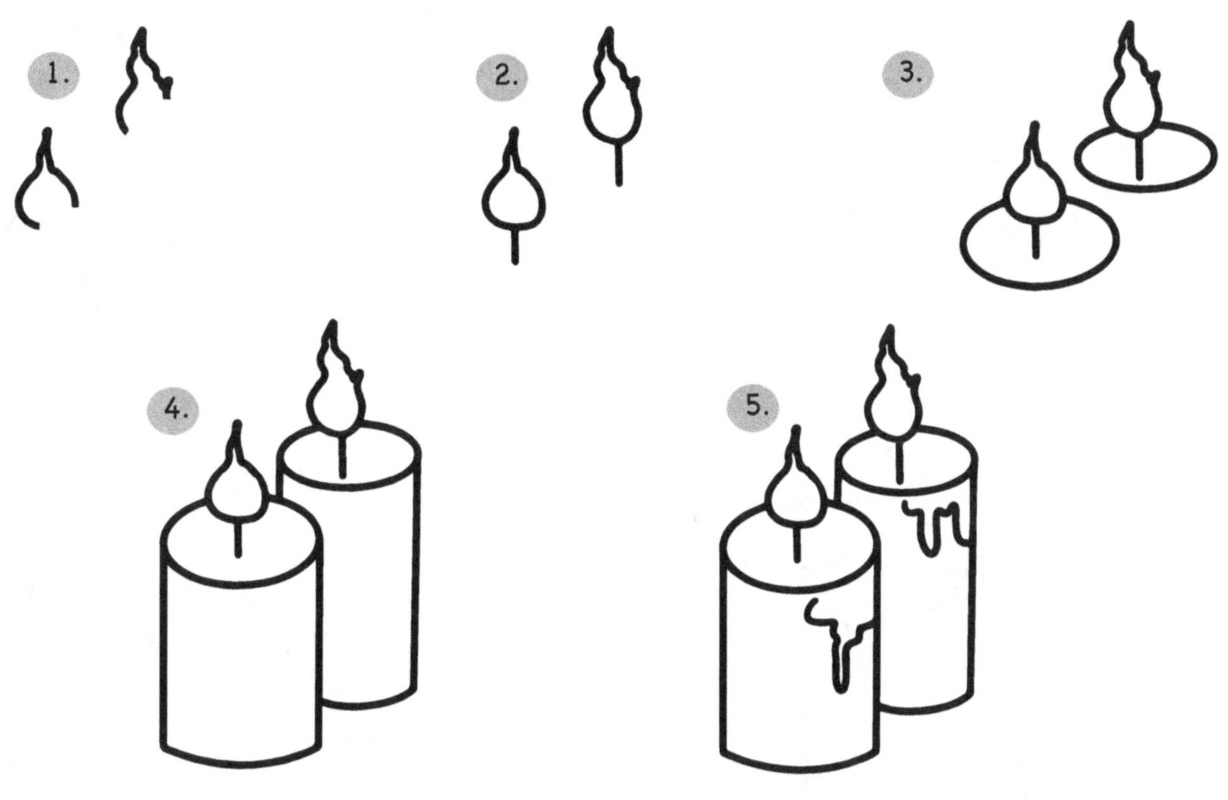

1.

2.

3.

4.

5.

Practice for drawing here.

Toothbrush and Toothpaste

1.

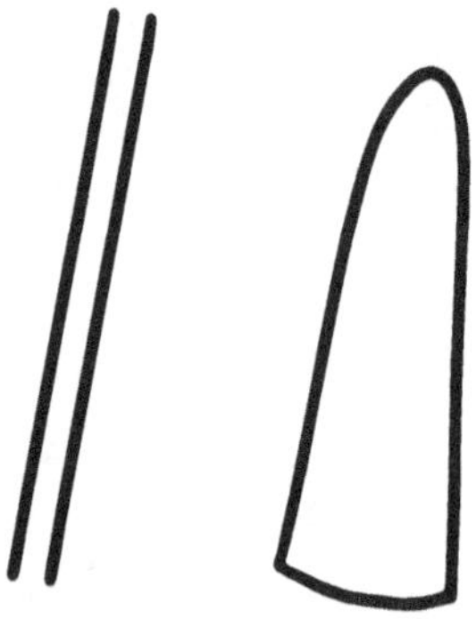

2.

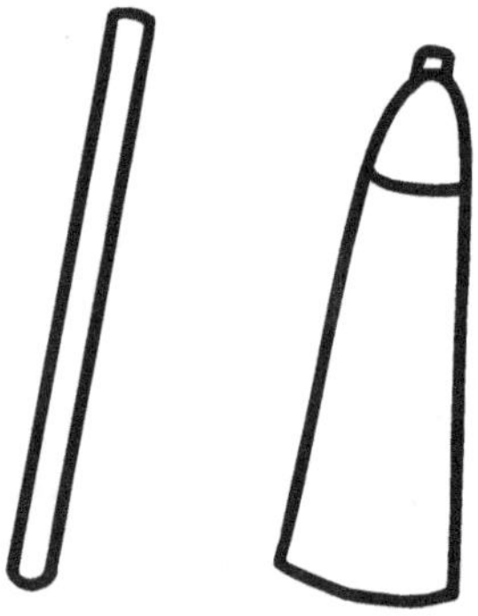

3.

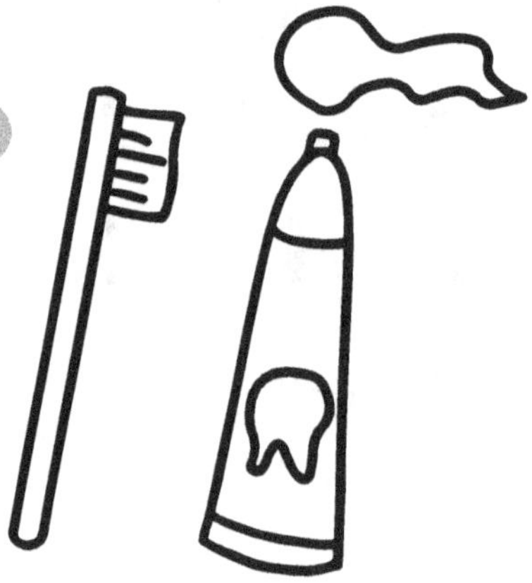

4.

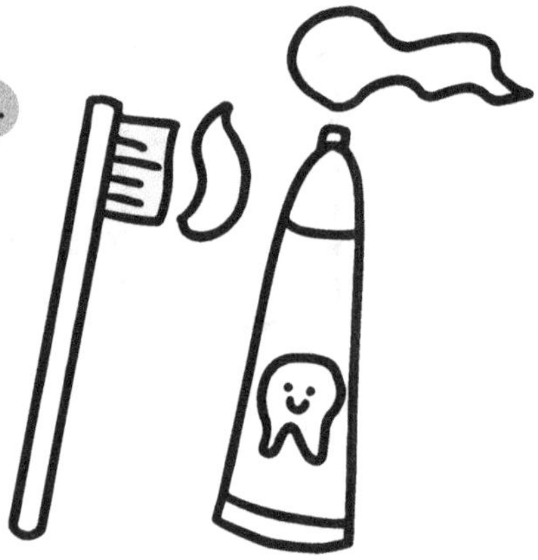

Practice for drawing here.

Umbrella

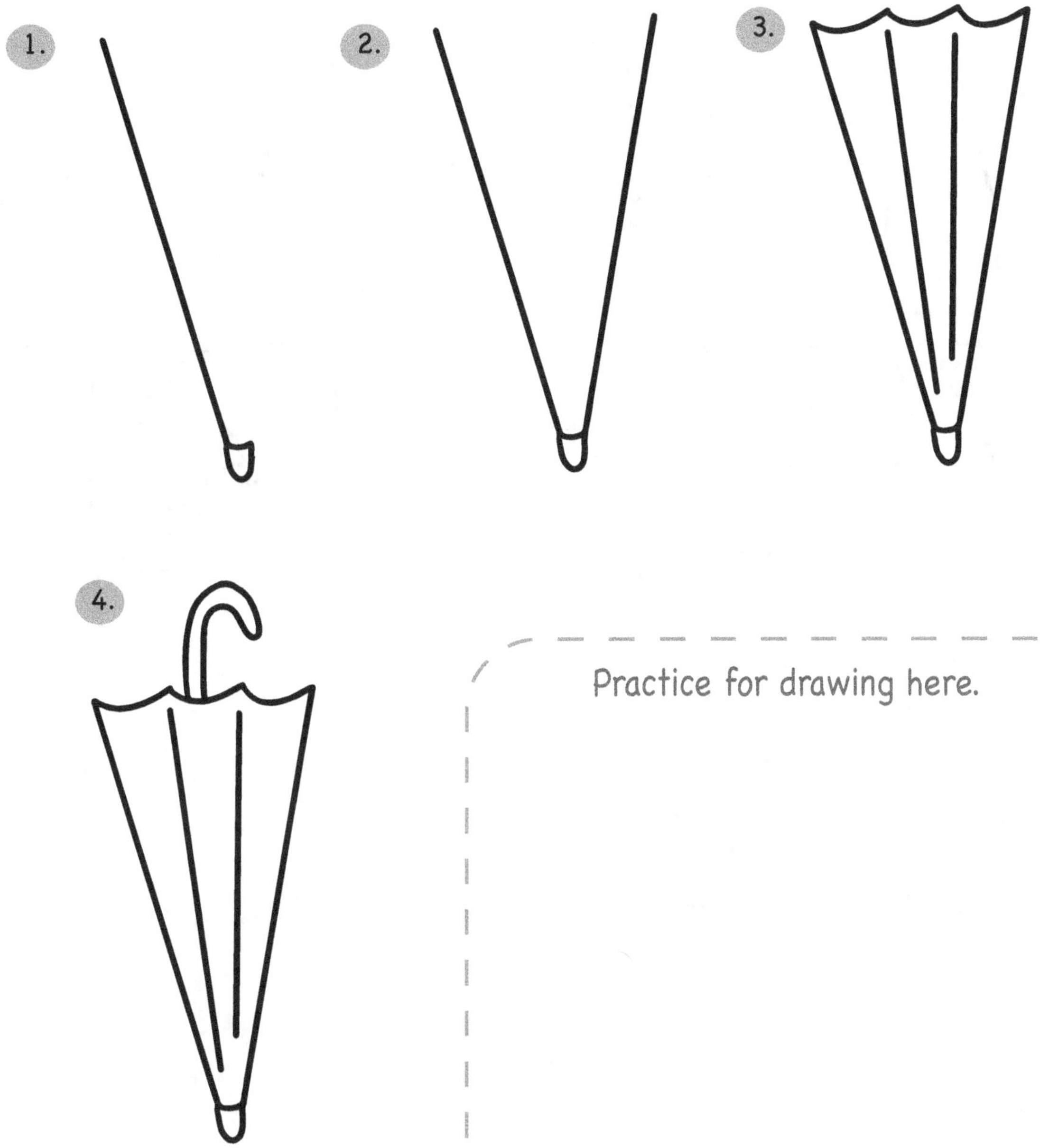

1.

2.

3.

4.

Practice for drawing here.

Window

1.

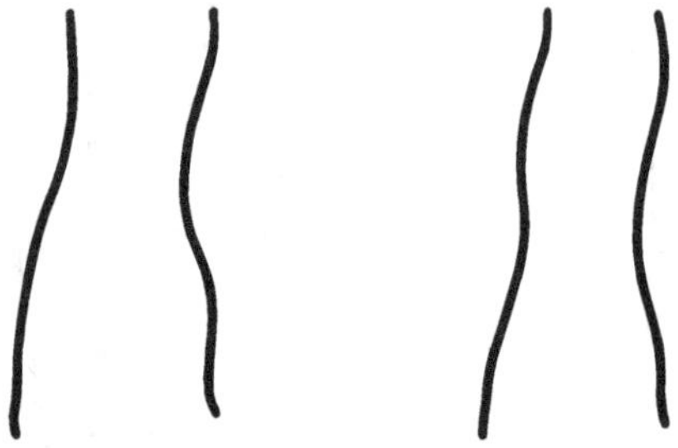

2.

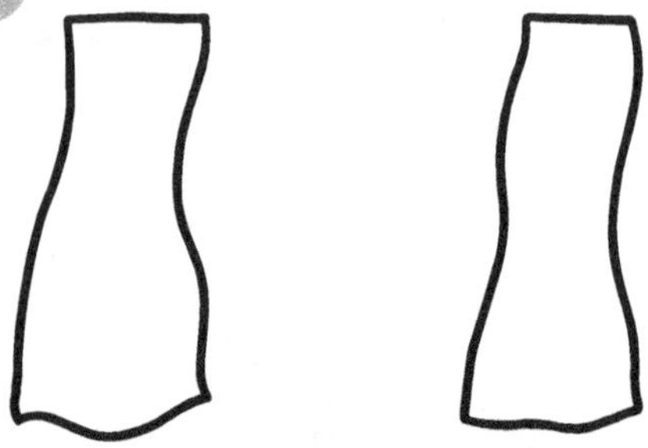

3.

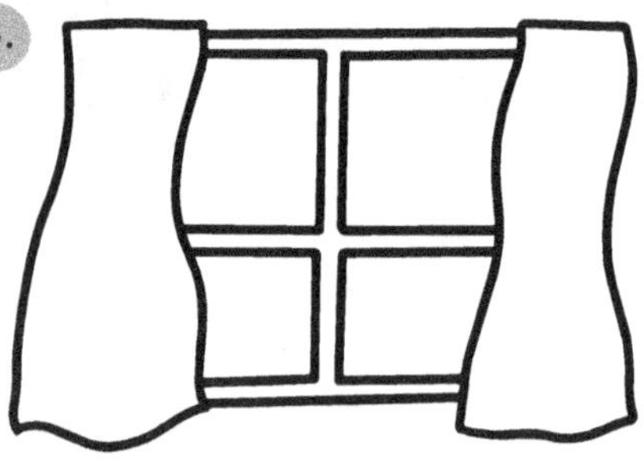

4.

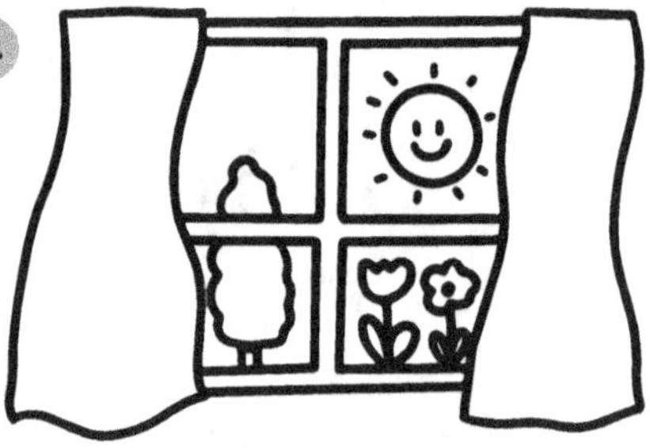

5.

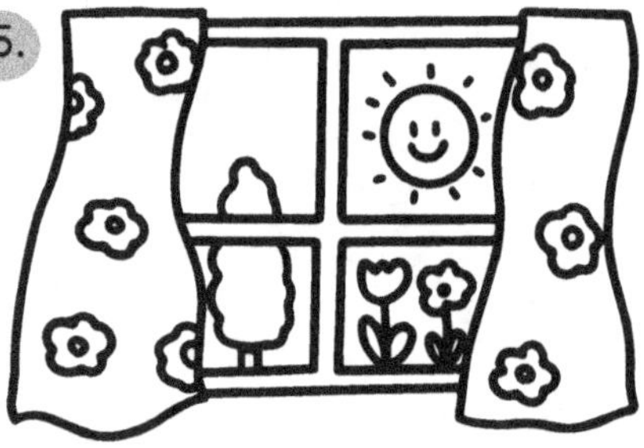

Practice for drawing here.

Toaster

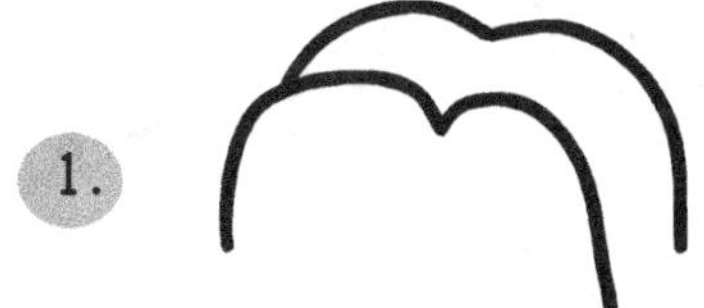

1.

2.

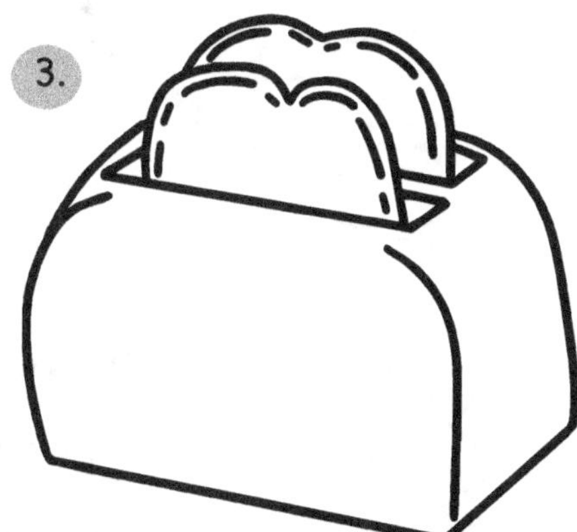

3.

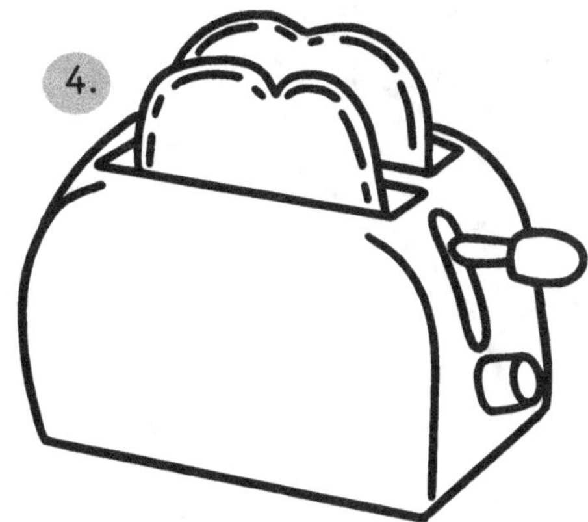

4.

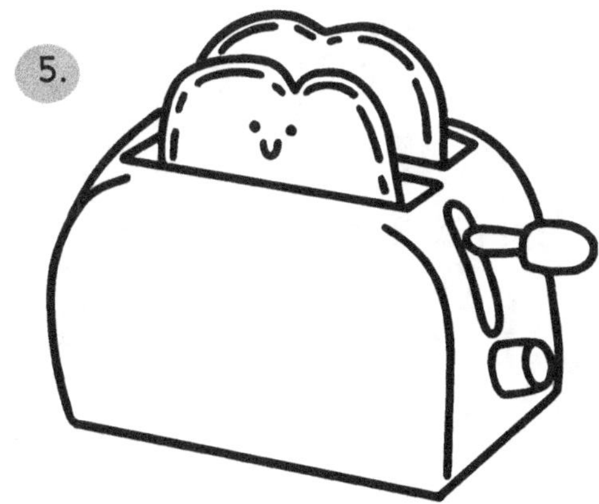

5.

Practice for drawing here.

Bed

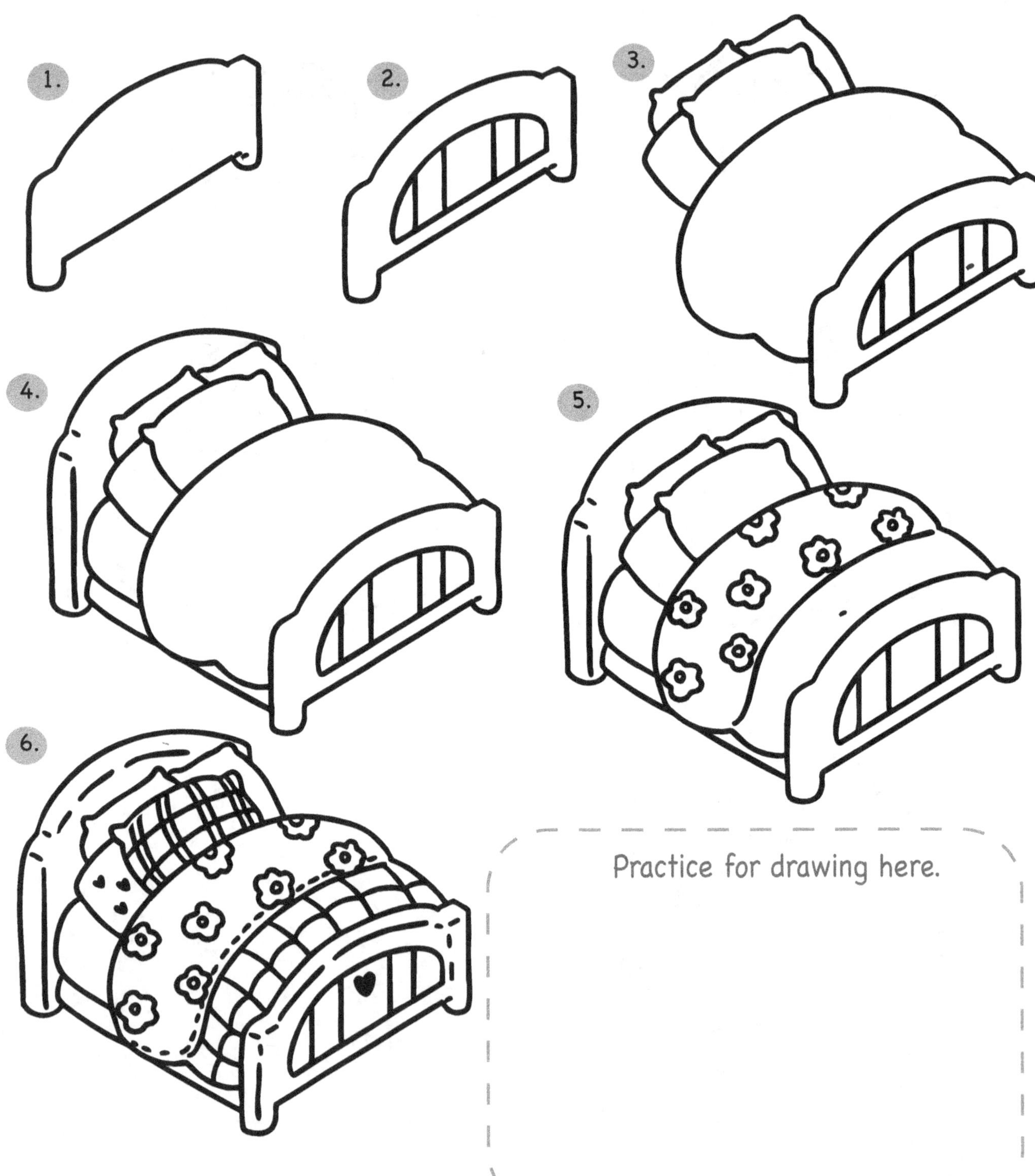

Picture frame

1.

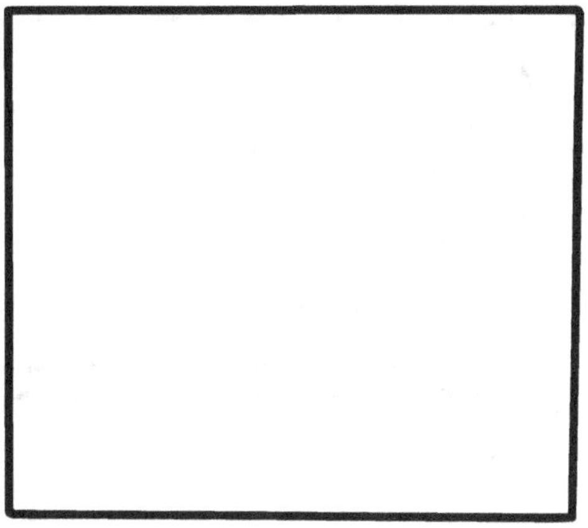

2.

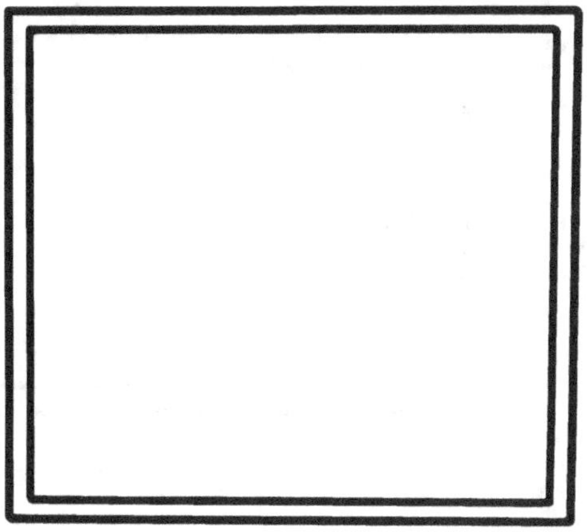

3.

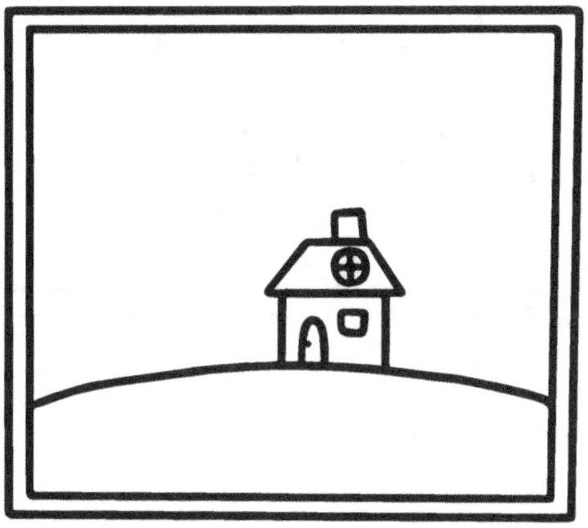

4.

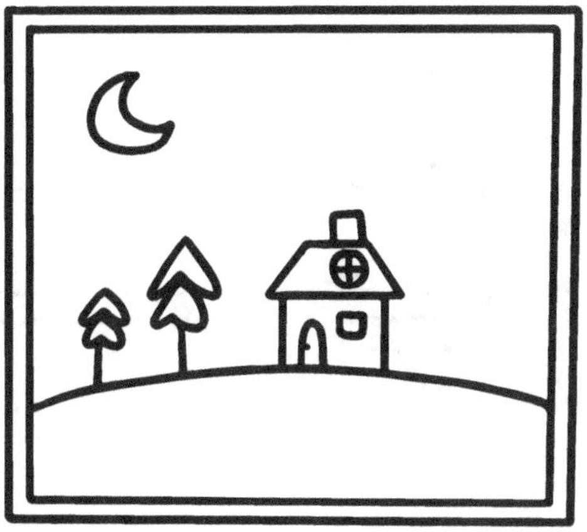

5.

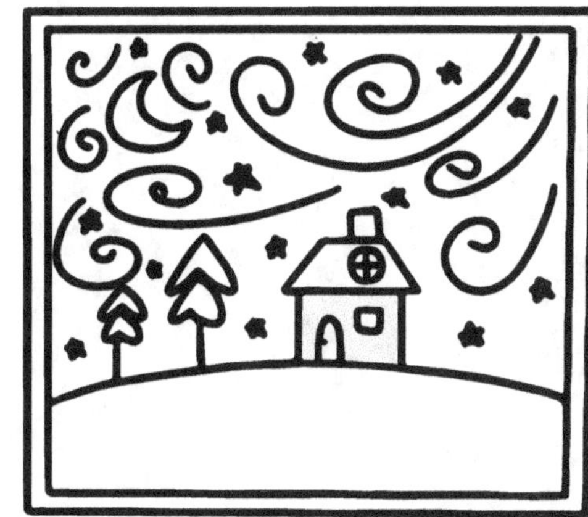

Practice for drawing here.

Radio

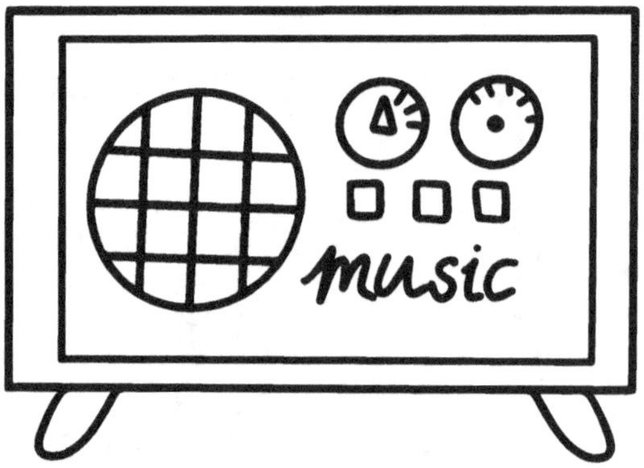

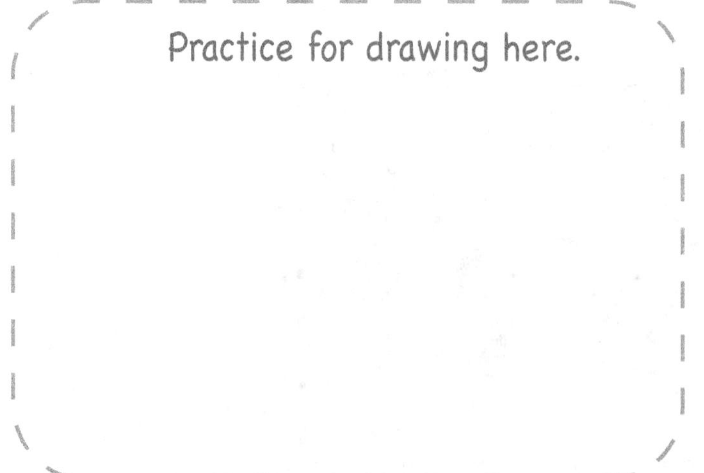

Practice for drawing here.

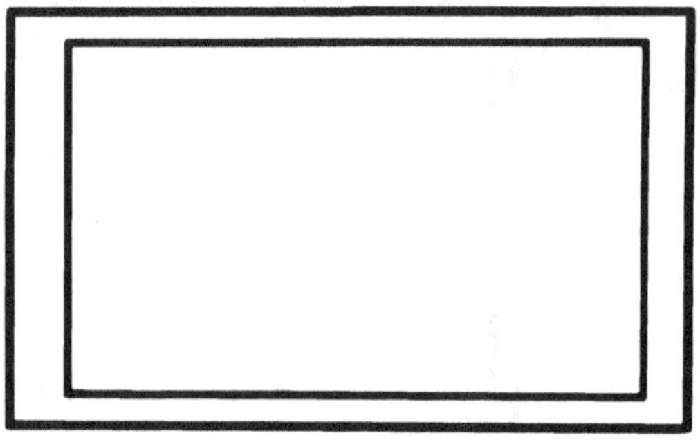

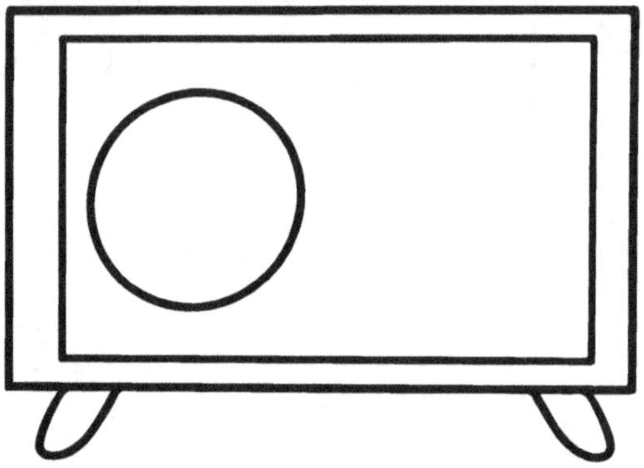

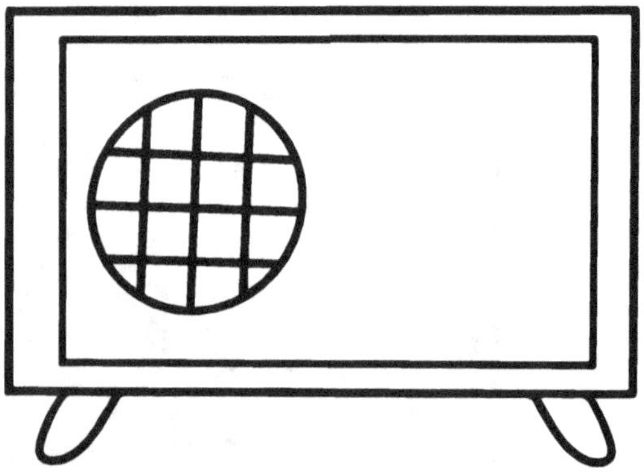

Fireplace

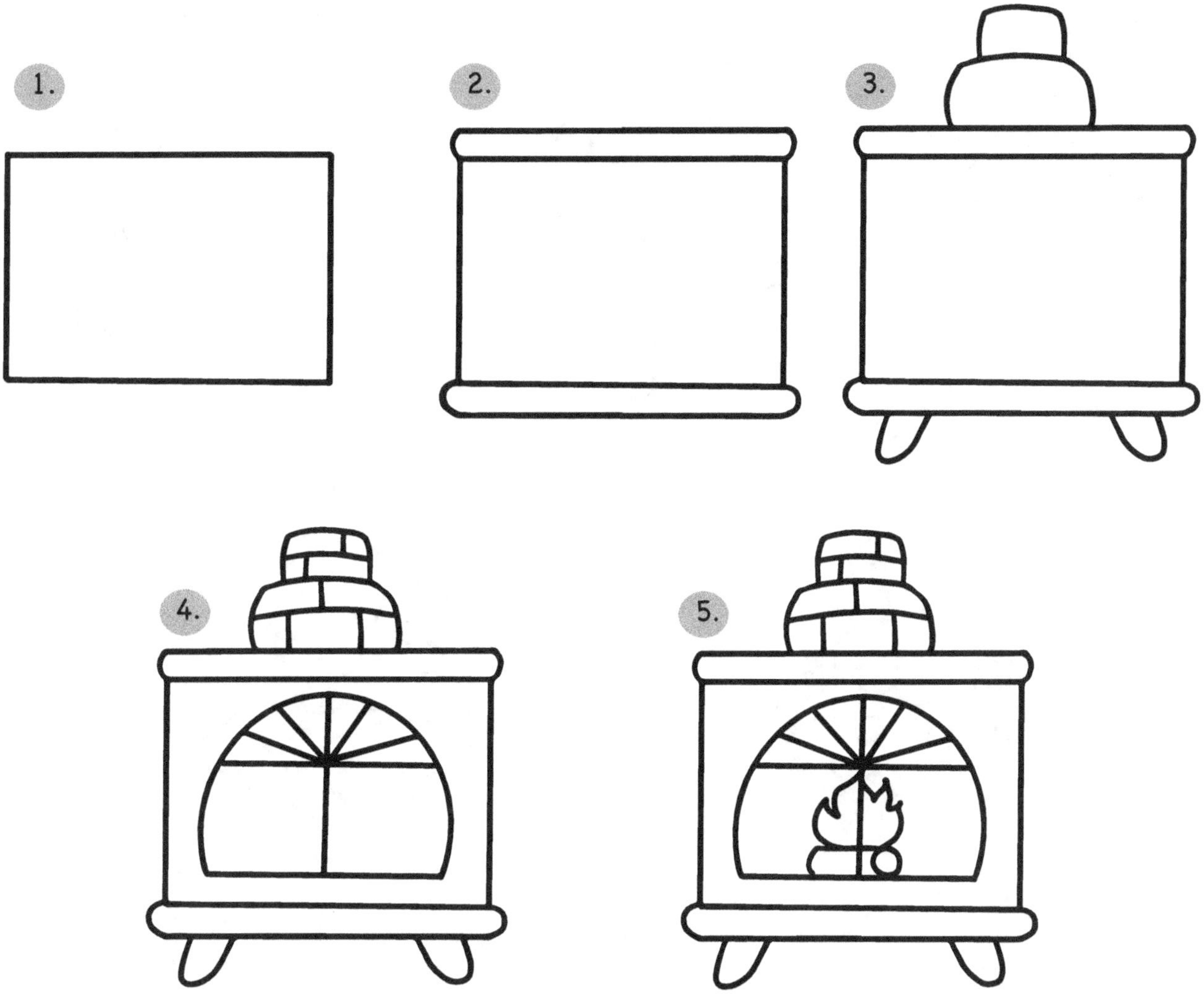

1.

2.

3.

4.

5.

Practice for drawing here.

Christmas Tree

1. 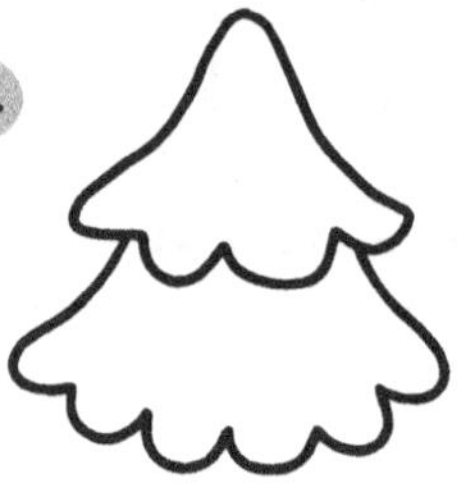
2. 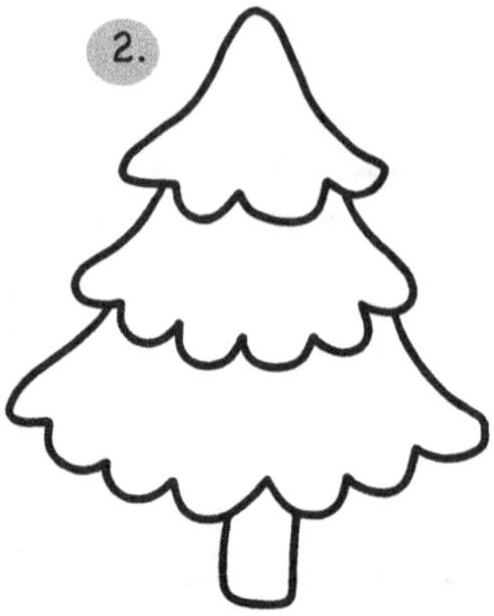
3. 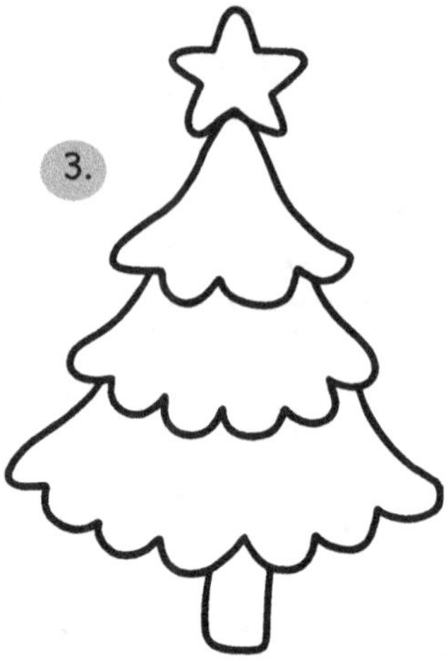
4. 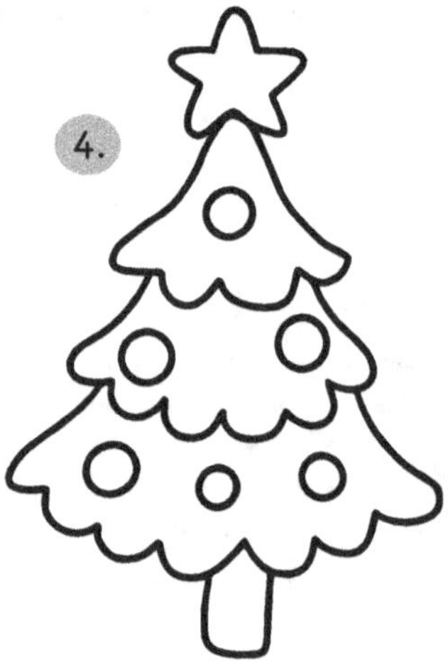
5.

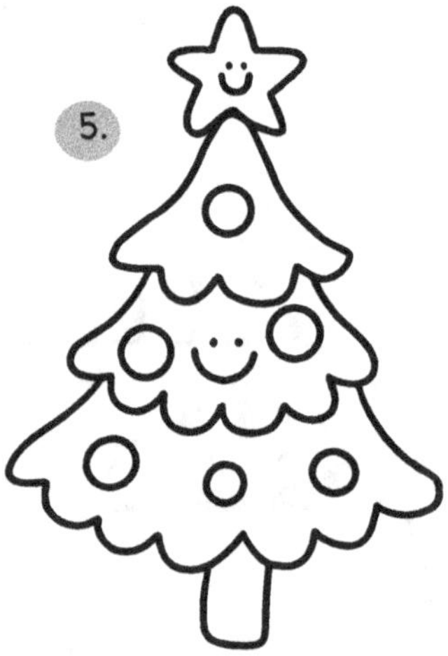

Practice for drawing here.

Bouquet

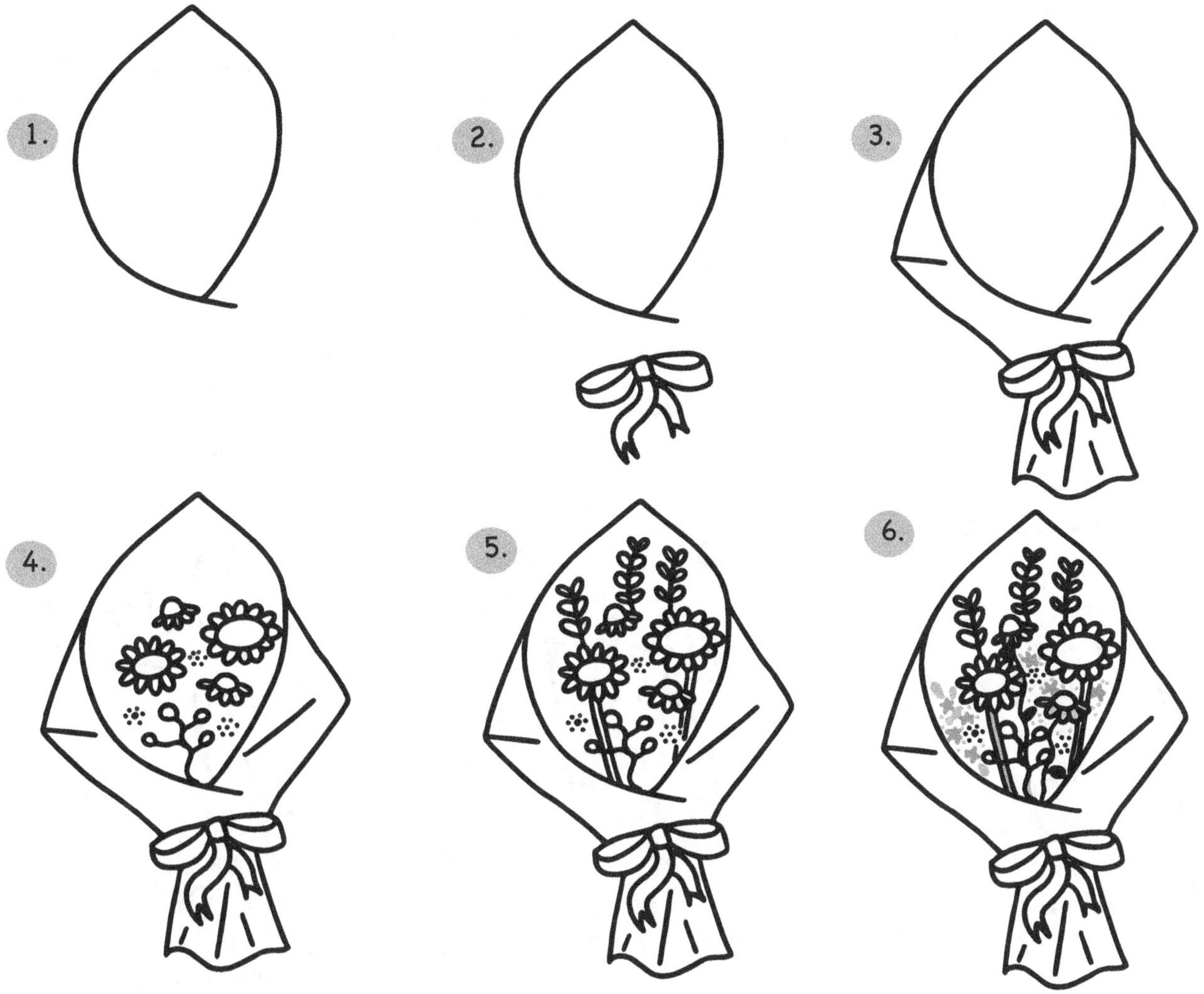

1.

2.

3.

4.

5.

6.

Practice for drawing here.

Calendar

1.

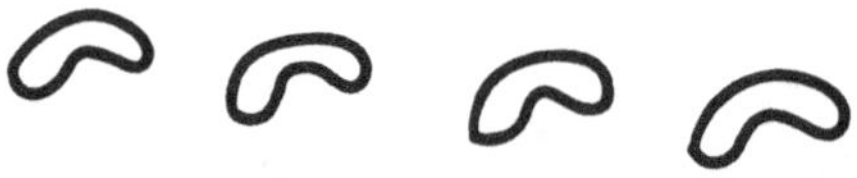

2.

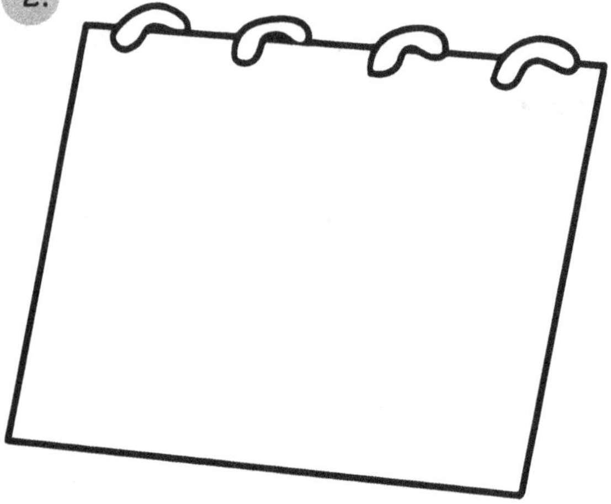

3.

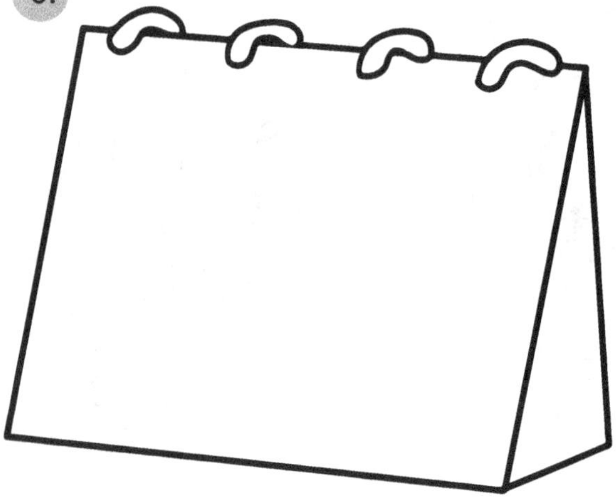

4.

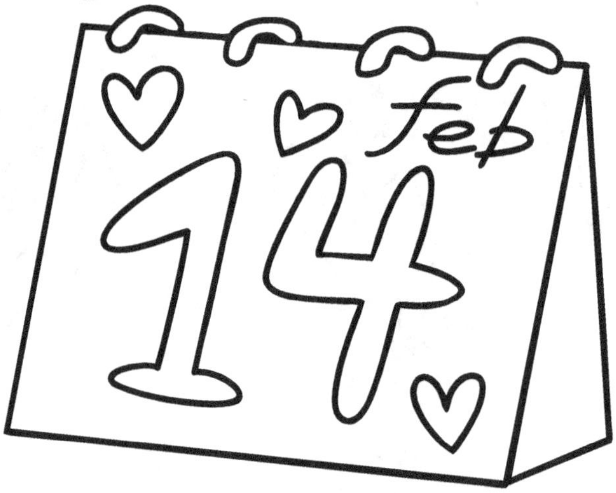

Practice for drawing here.

Teddy Bear

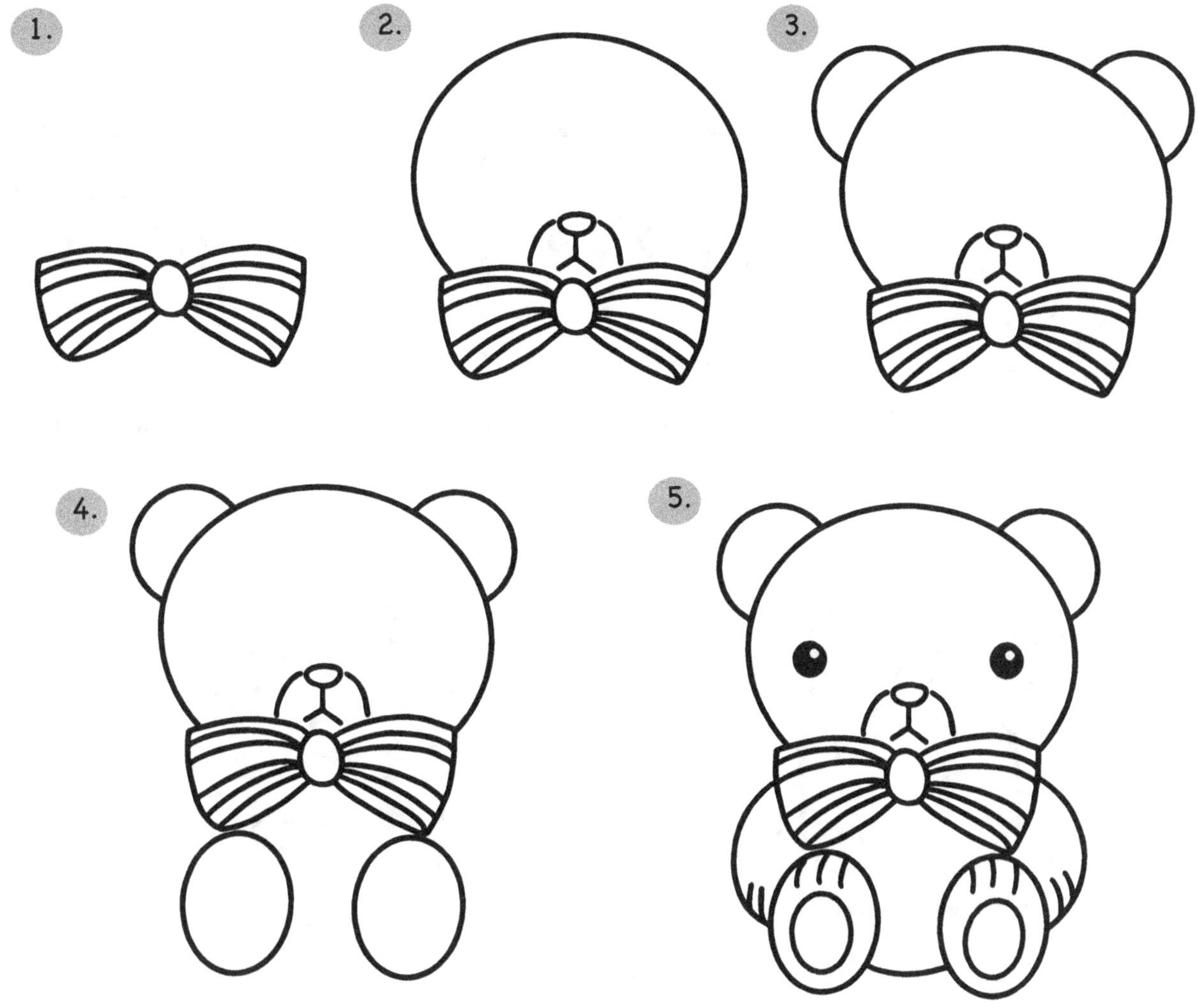

1.

2.

3.

4.

5.

Practice for drawing here.

Perfume

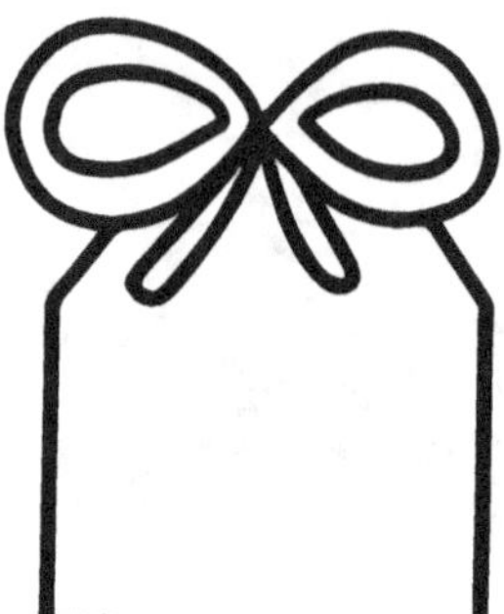

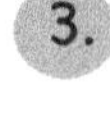

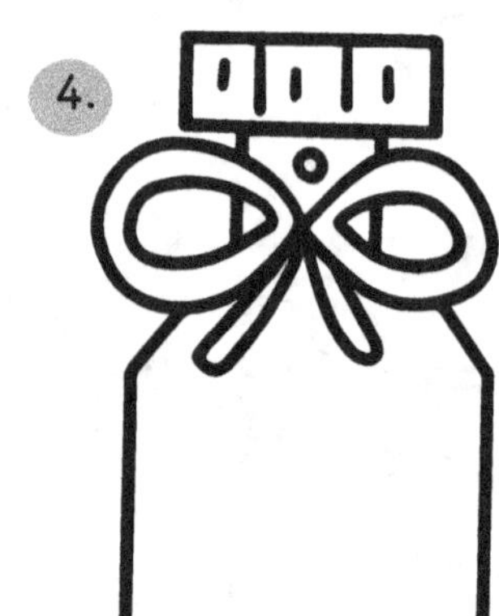

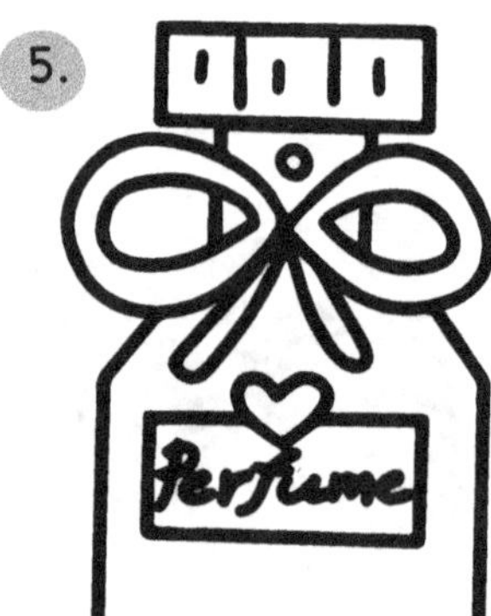

Practice for drawing here.

Lipstick

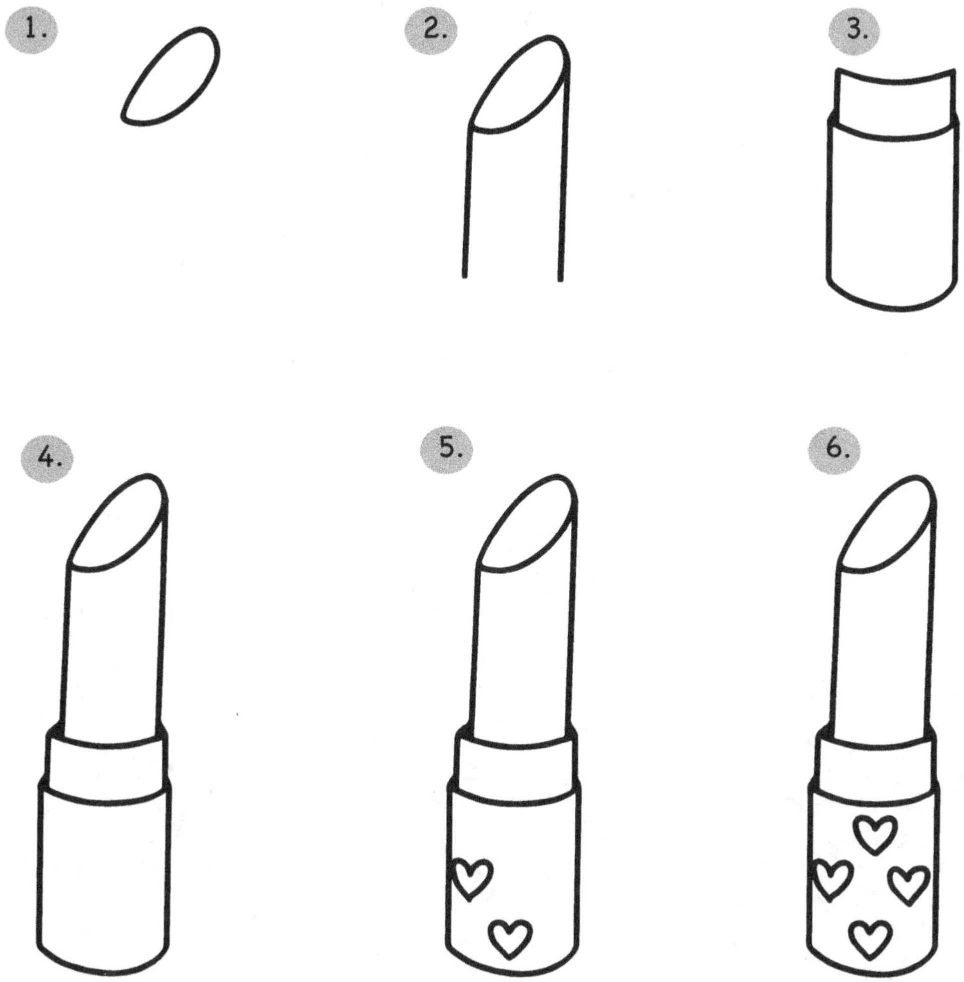

1.

2.

3.

4.

5.

6.

Practice for drawing here.

Telephone

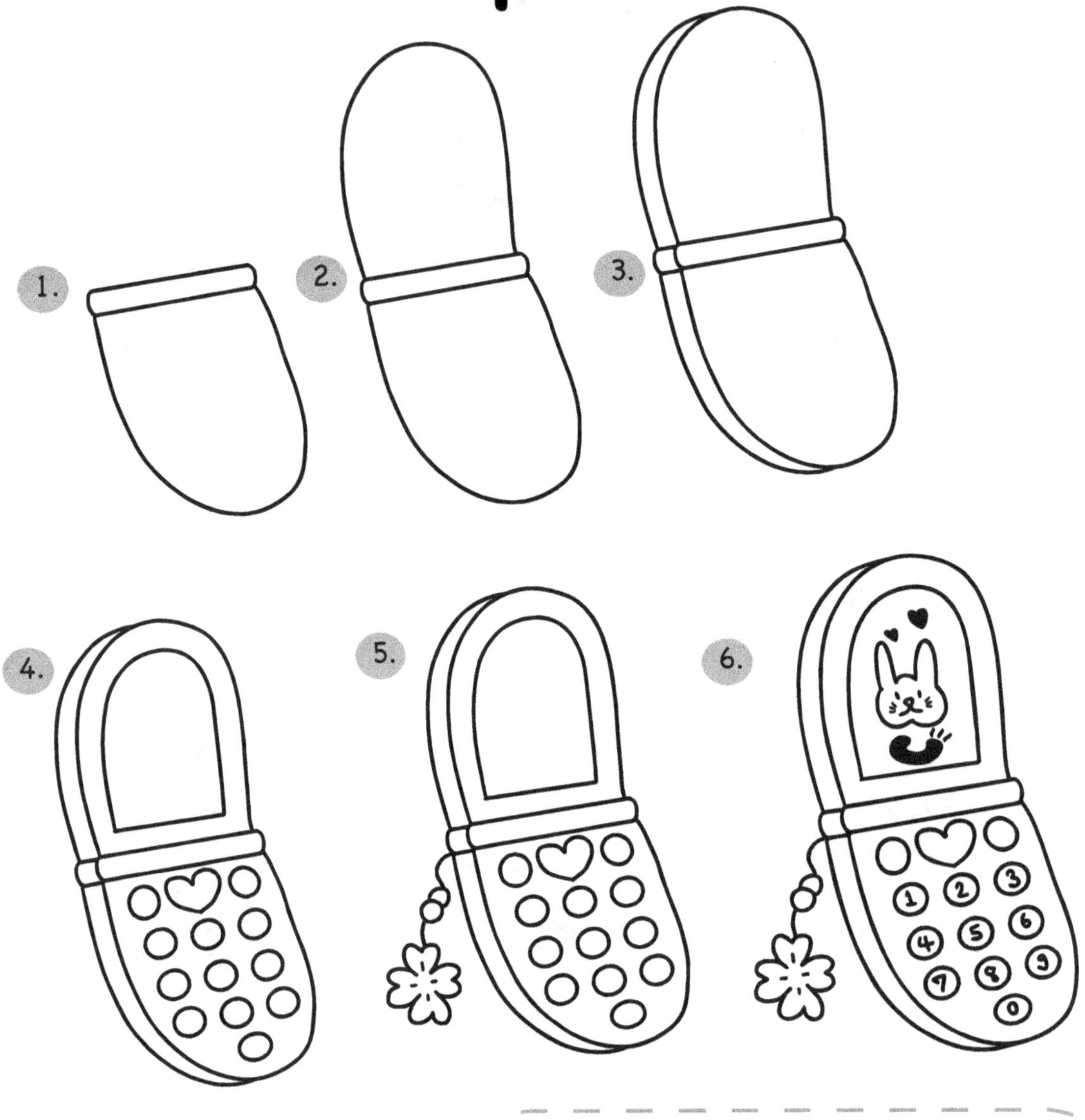

1.

2.

3.

4.

5.

6.

Practice for drawing here.

Oven Gloves

1.

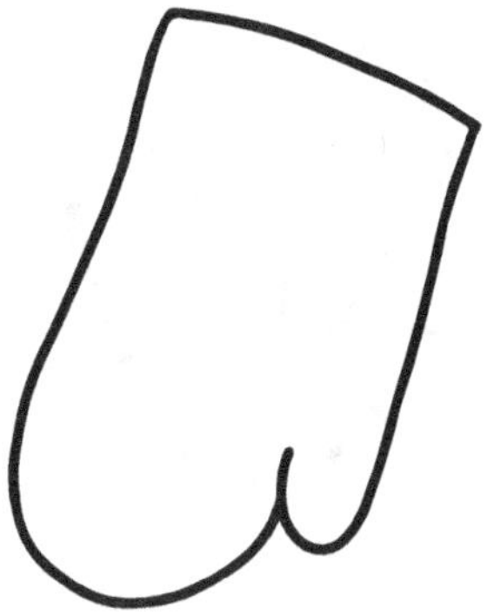

2.

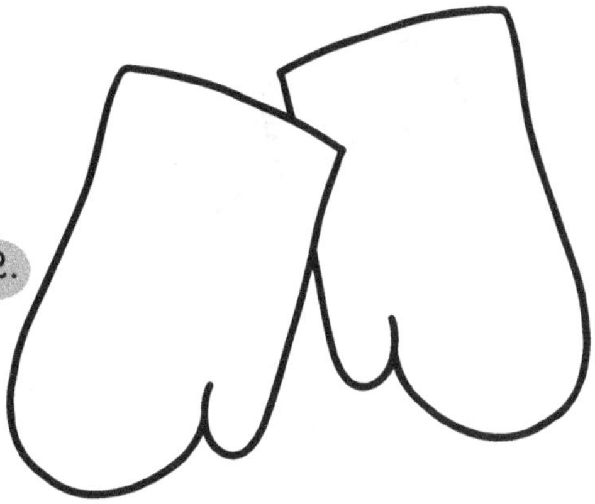

3.

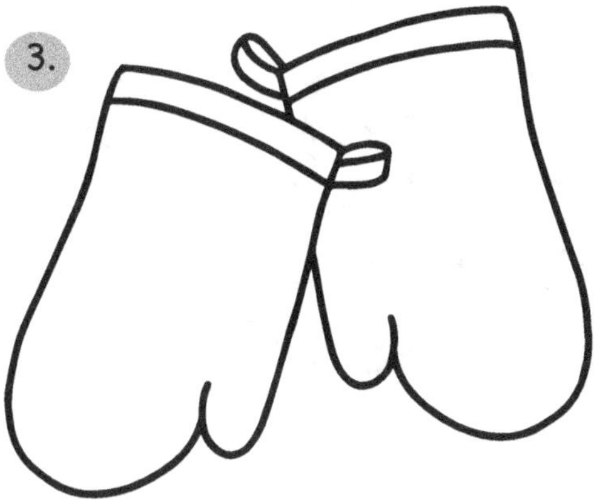

4.

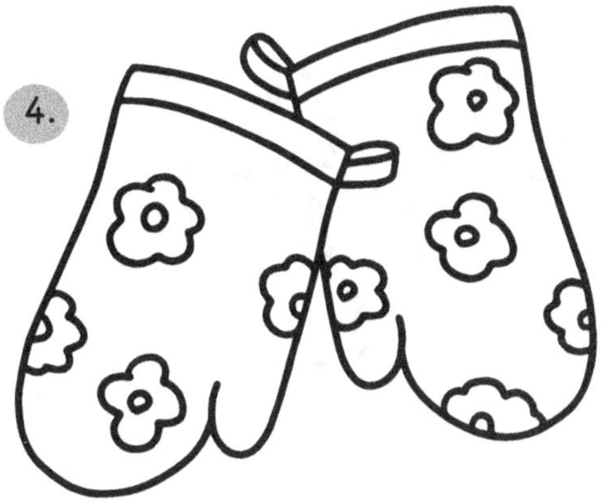

Practice for drawing here.

Sleepers

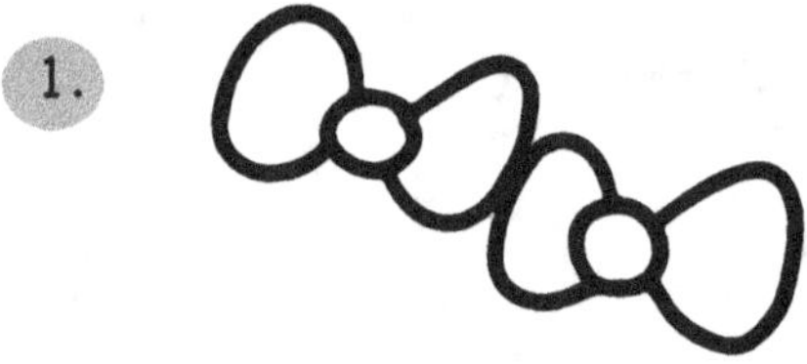

1.

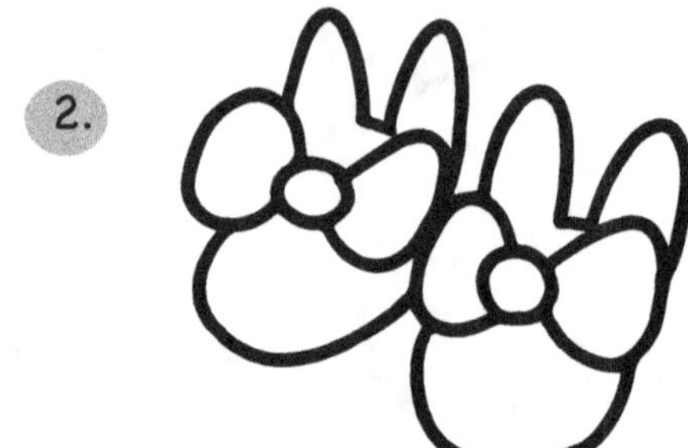

2.

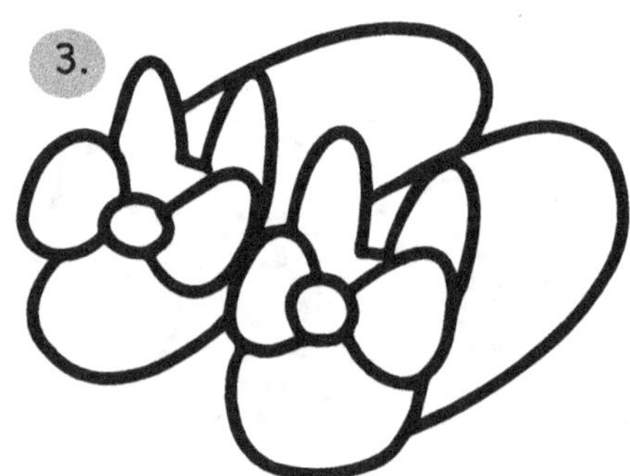

3.

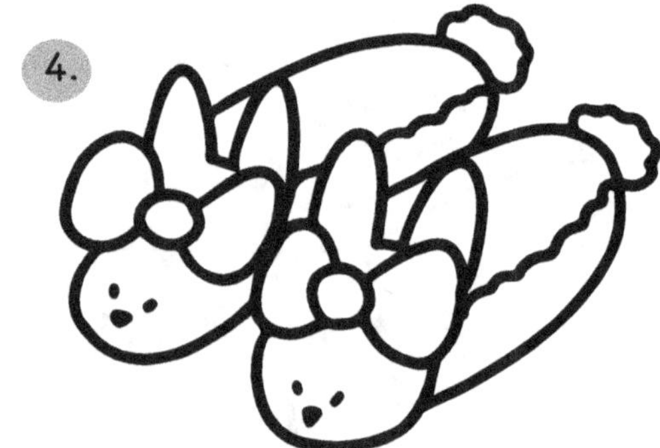

4.

Practice for drawing here.

Toy house

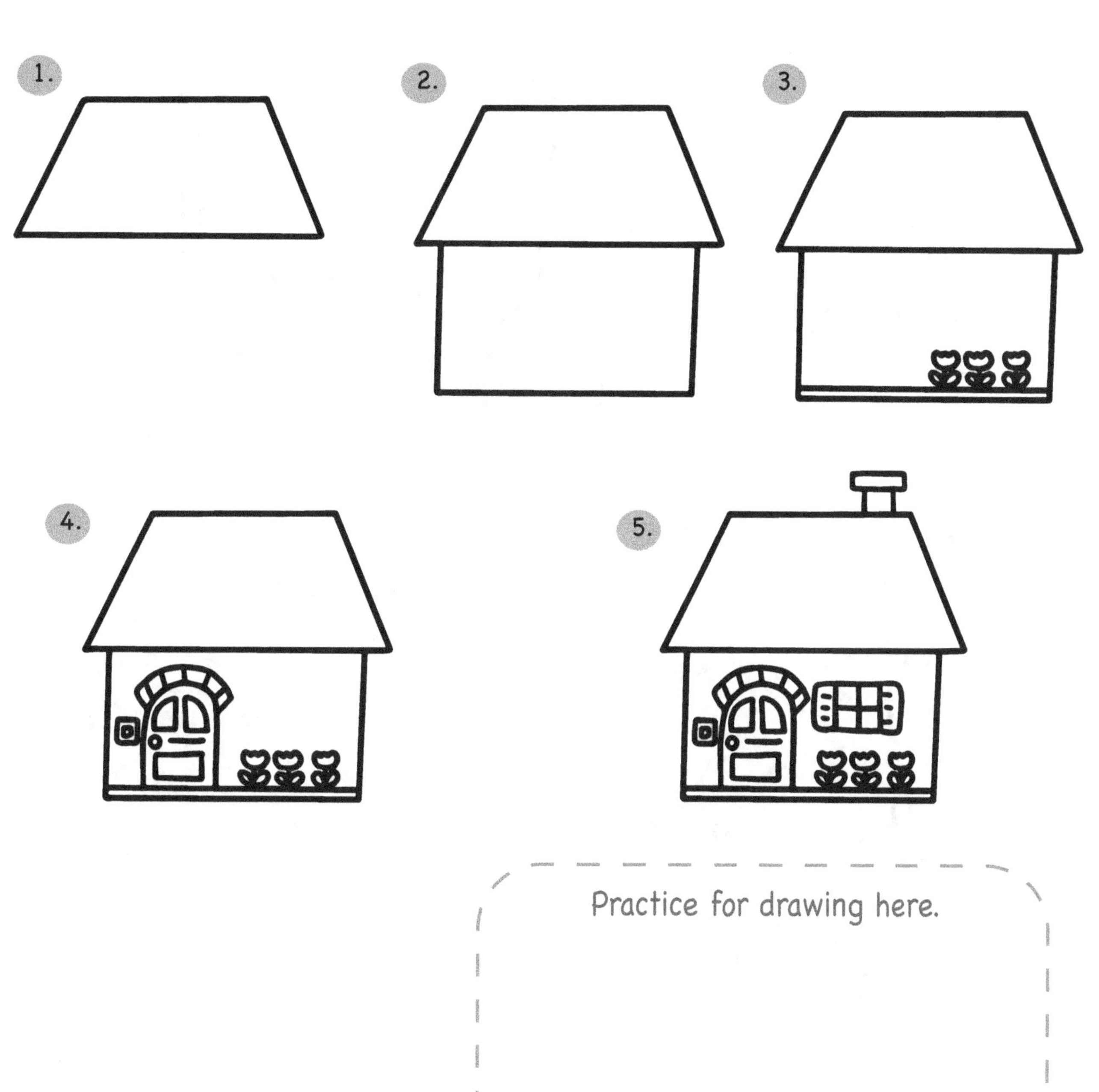

Practice for drawing here.

Broom

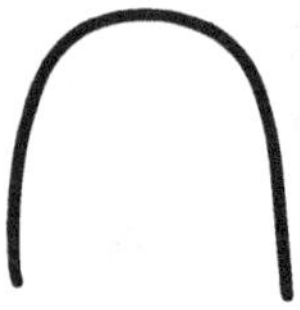

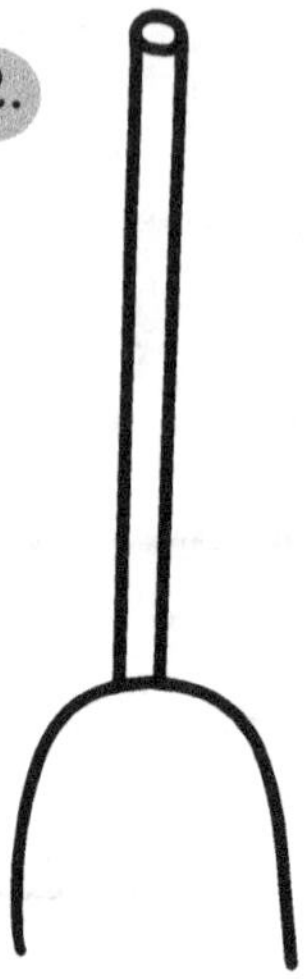

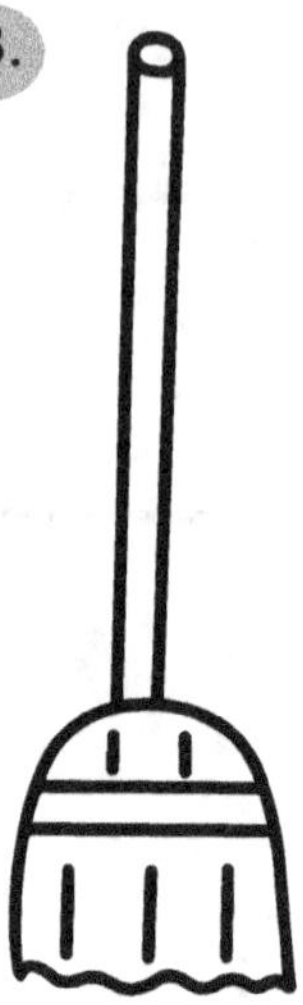

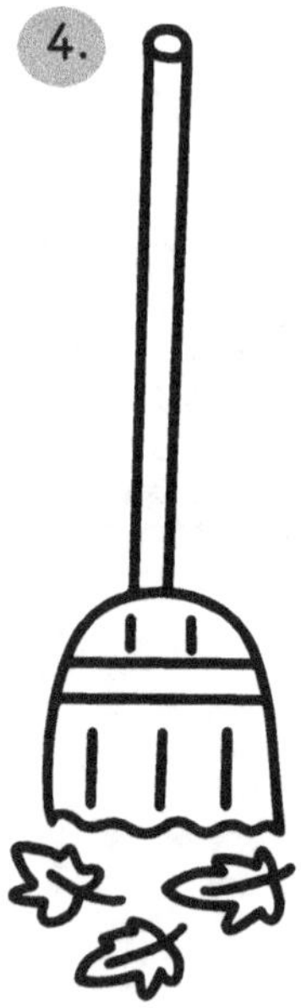

Mirror

1. 2. 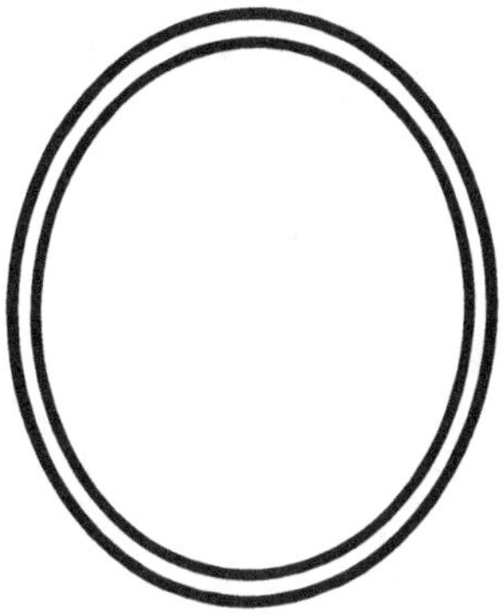 3.

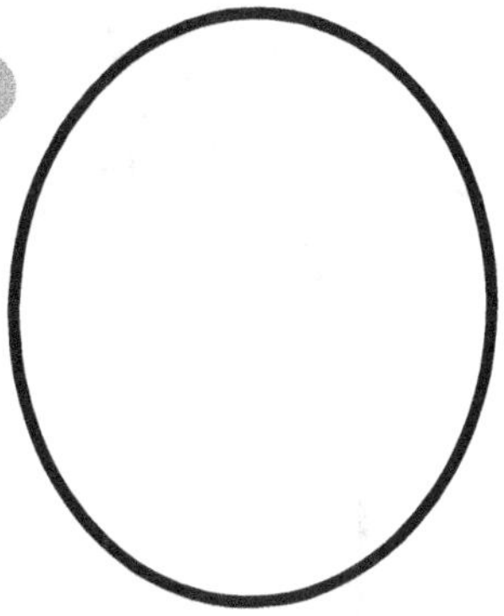

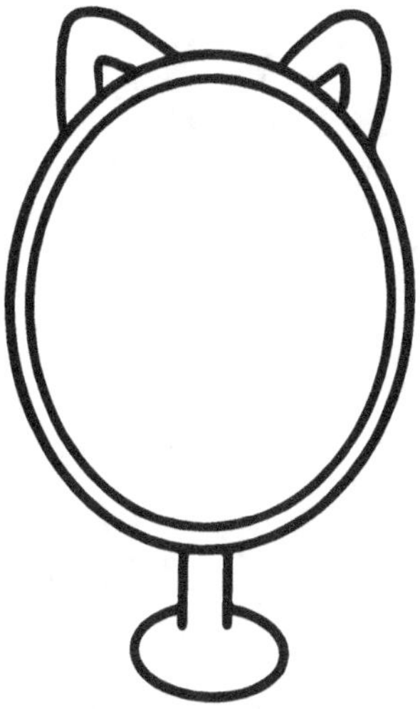

4. 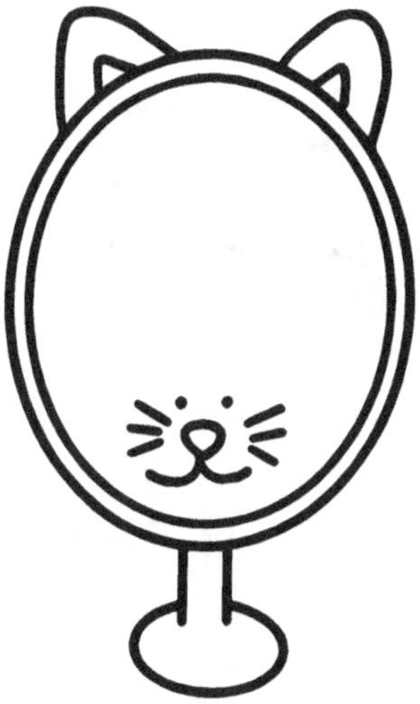 Practice for drawing here.

Shampoo

1. 2. 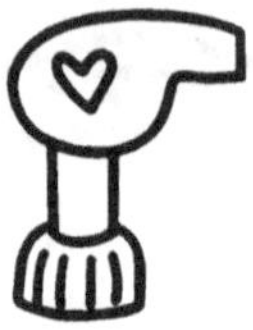 3.

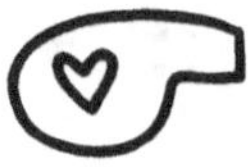

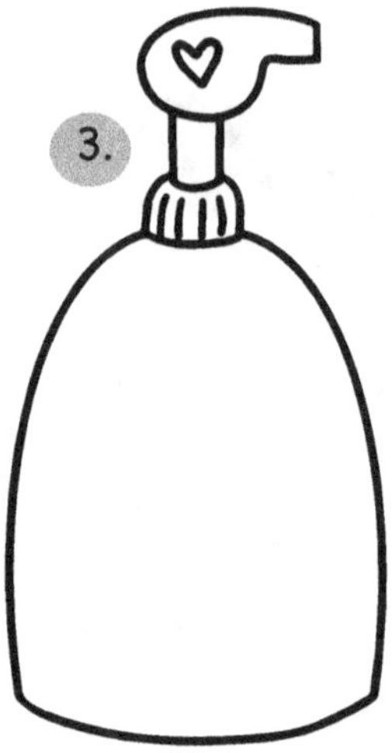

4.

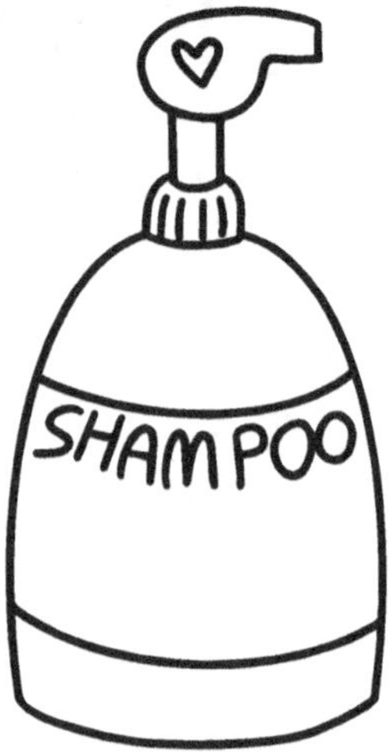

5.

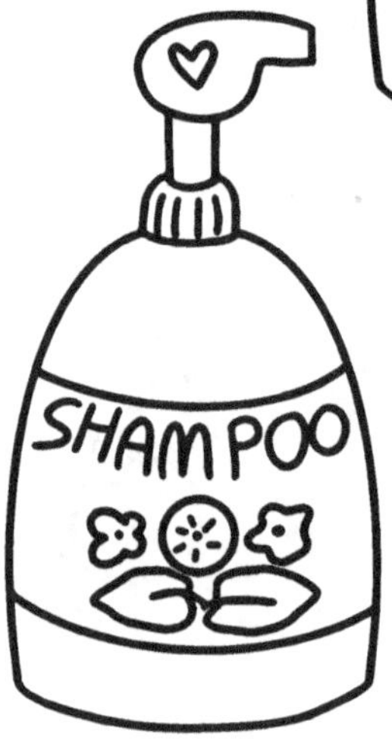

Practice for drawing here.

Sunscreen

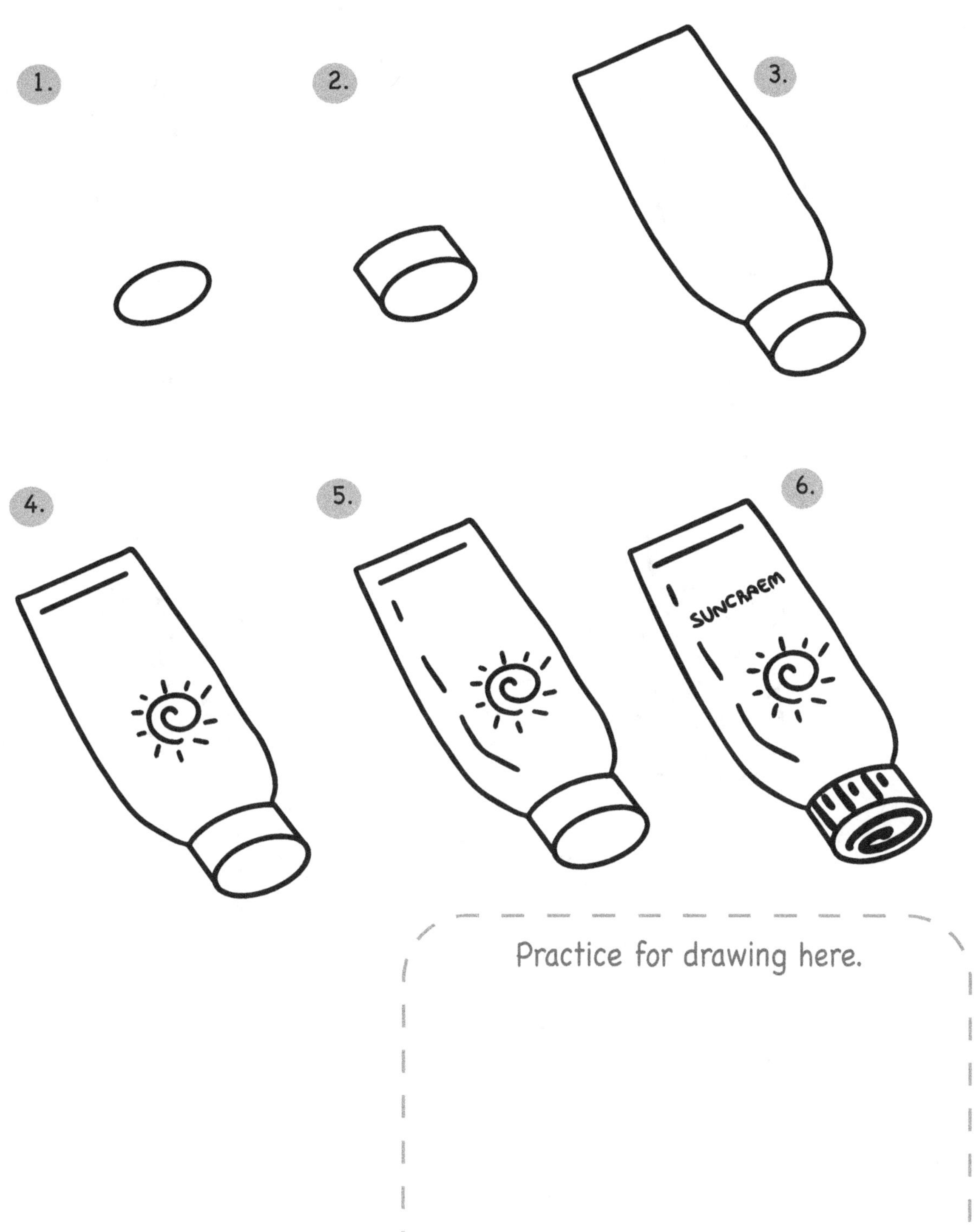

Practice for drawing here.

Honey Bear

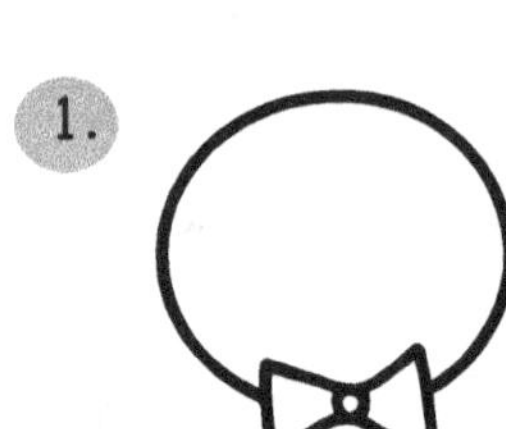

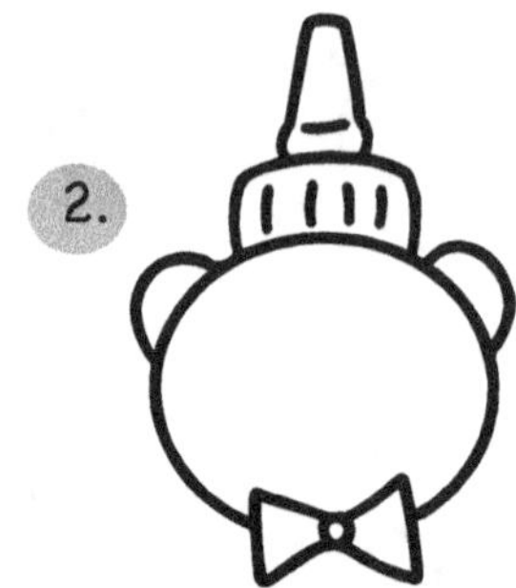

Practice for drawing here.

Strawberry Jam

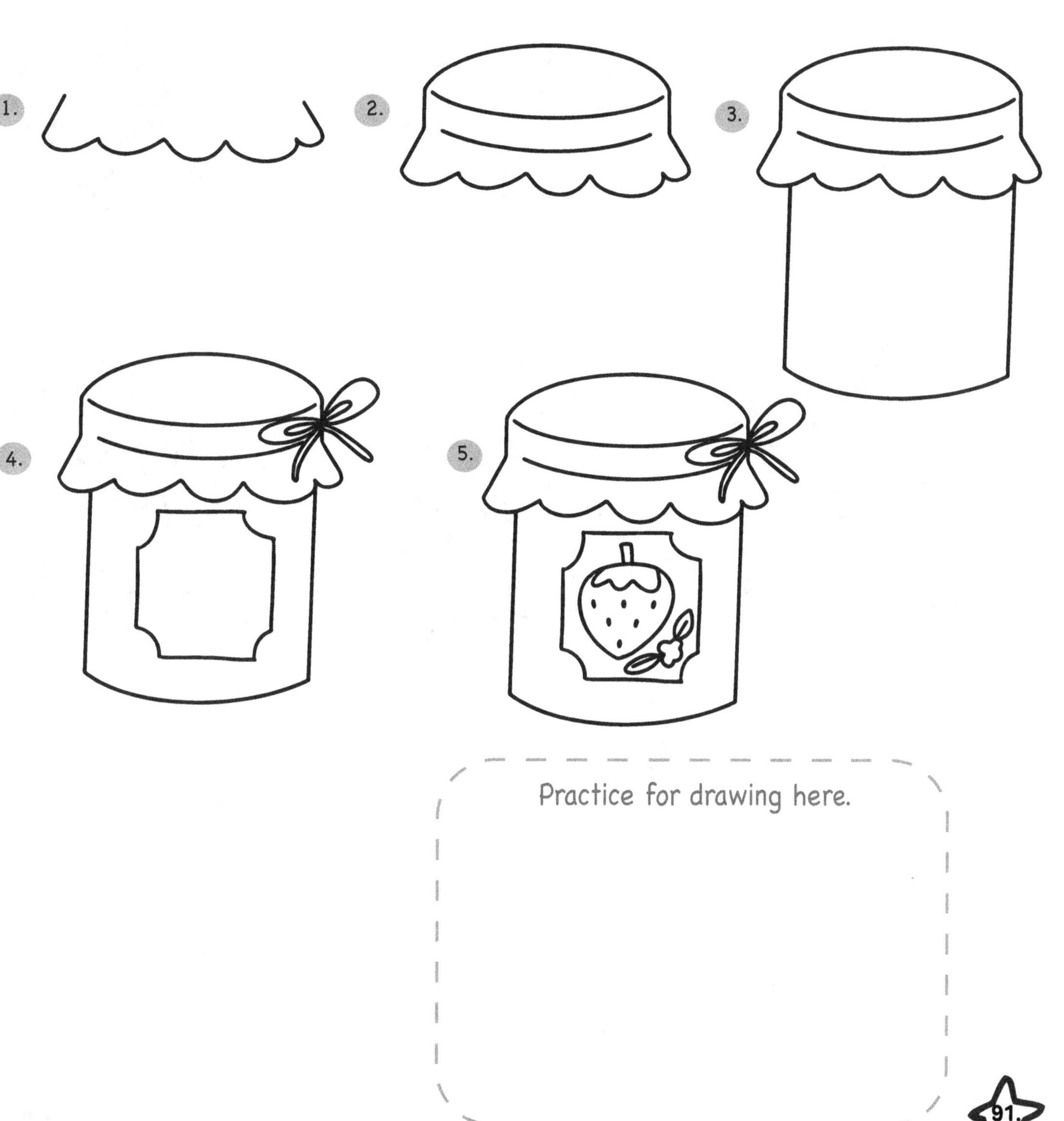

Daisy

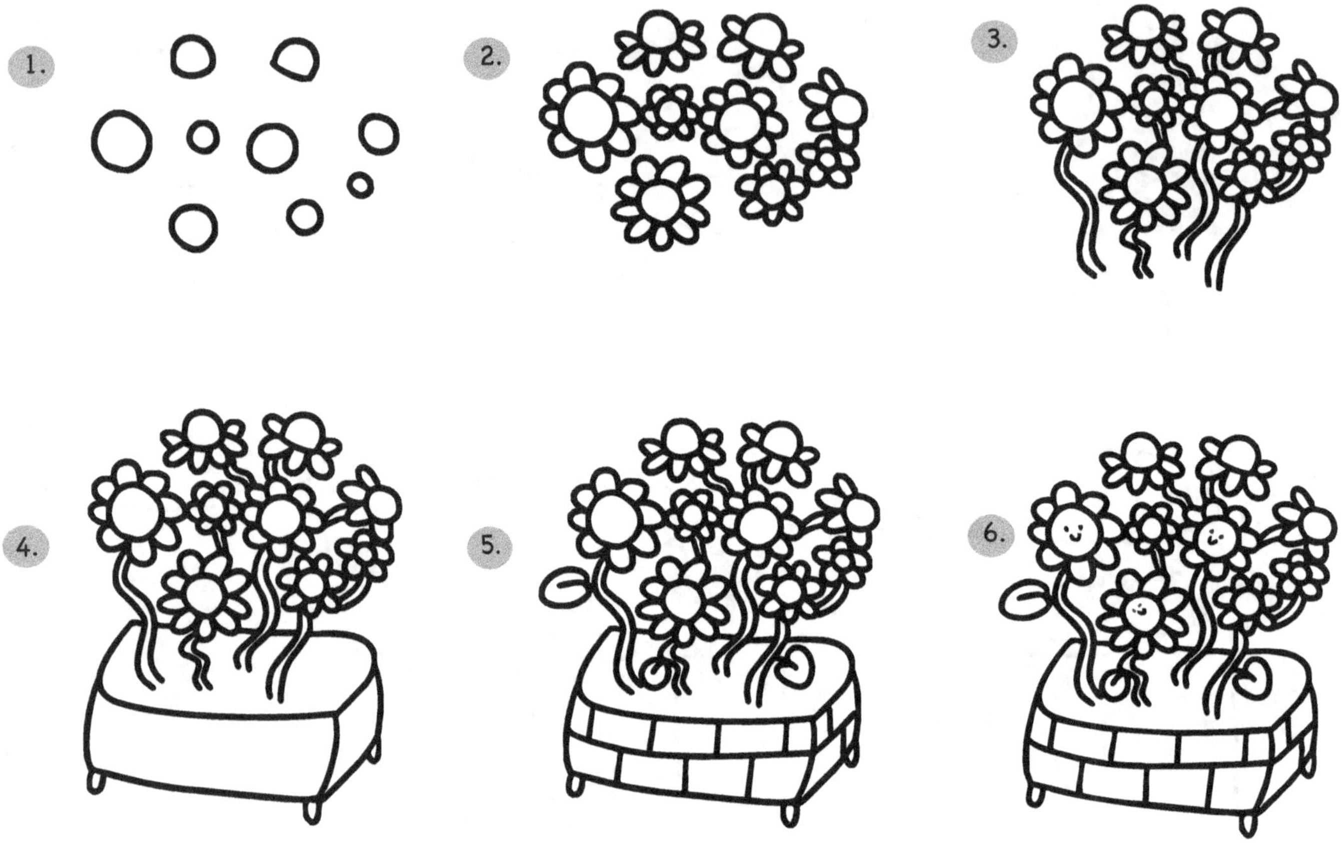

1. 2. 3.

4. 5. 6.

Practice for drawing here.

Rose

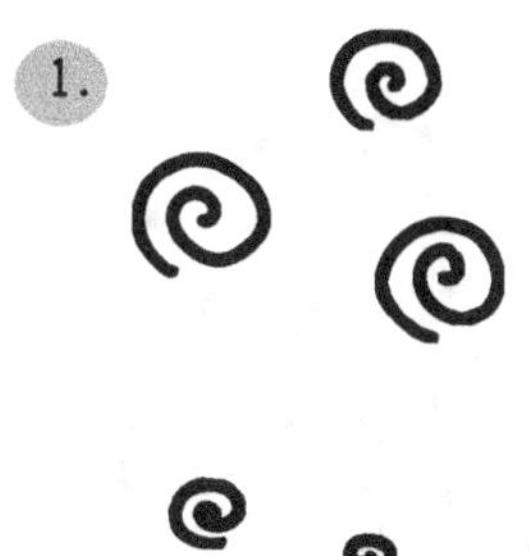

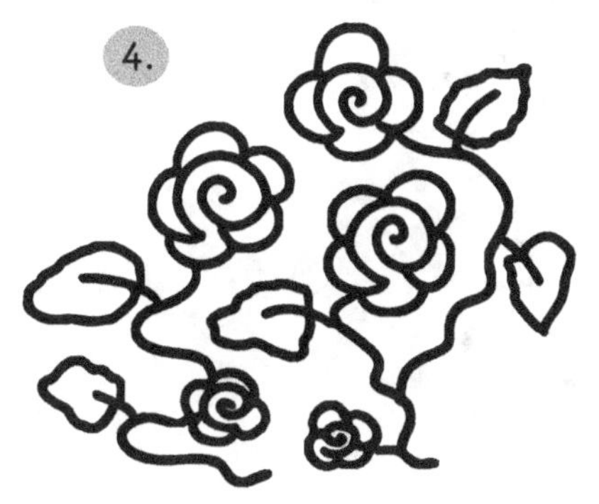

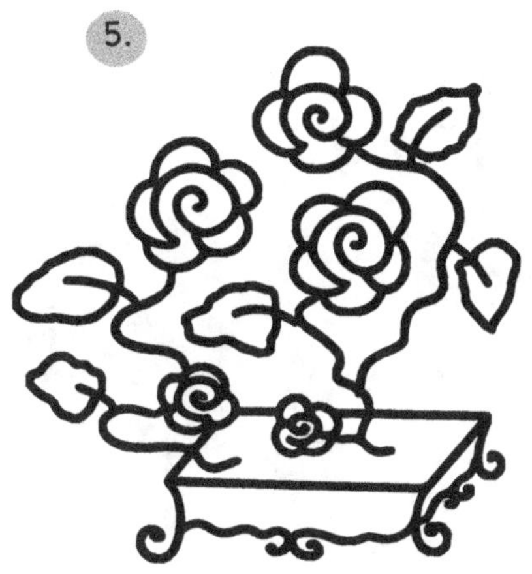

Practice for drawing here.

Sunflower

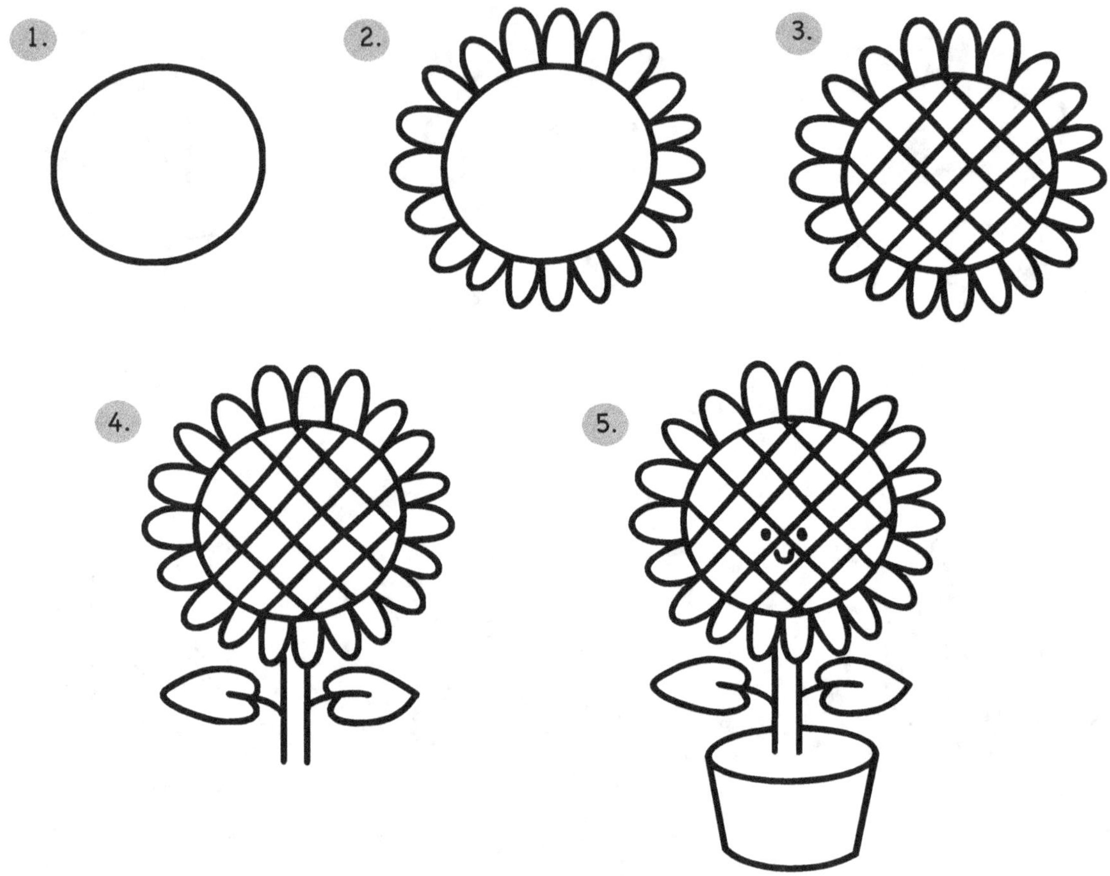

1.
2.
3.
4.
5.

Practice for drawing here.

Tulips

1. 2. 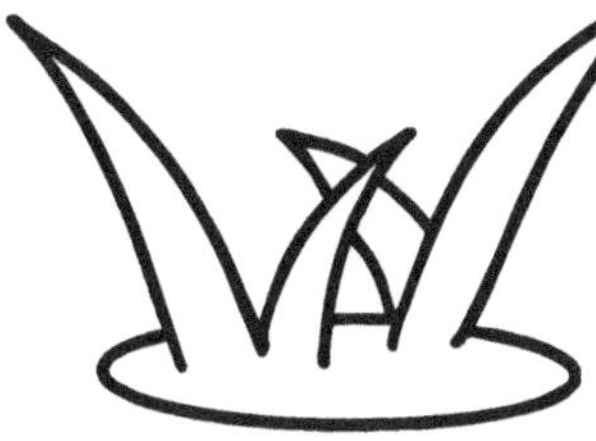 3.

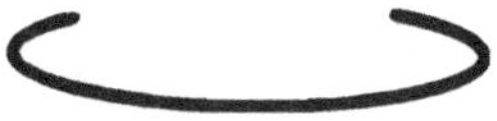

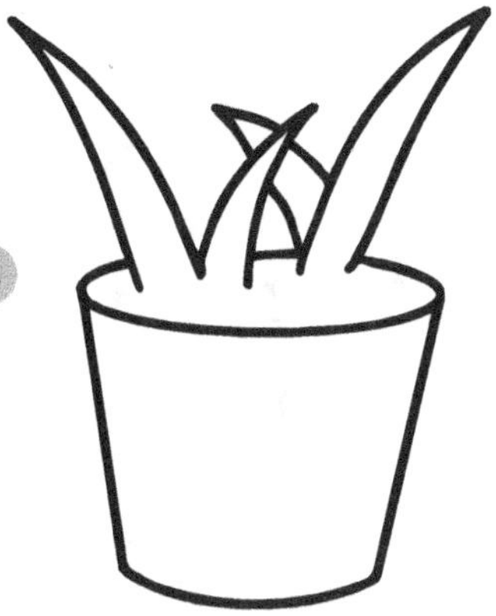

4. 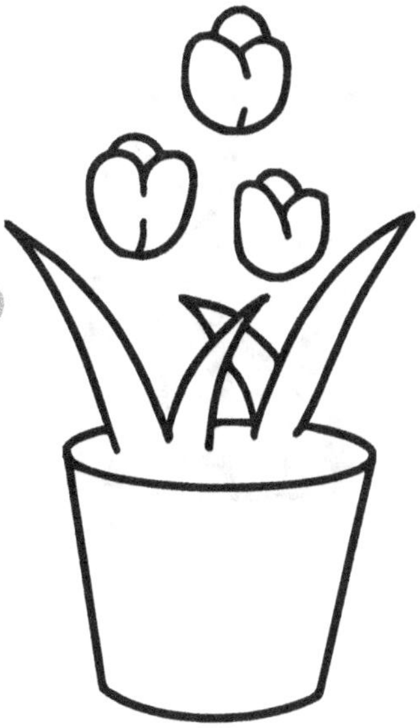 5. 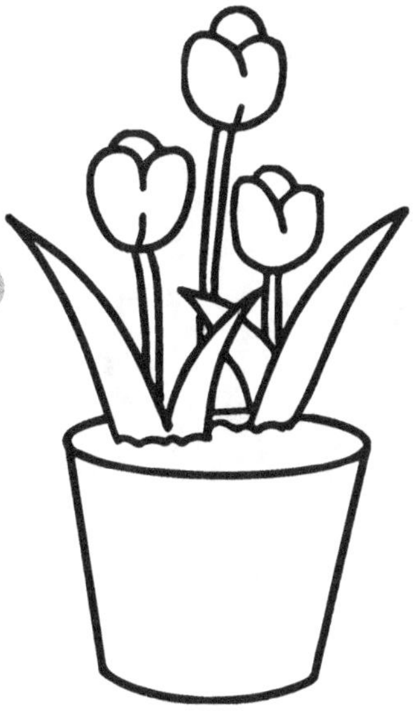 6.

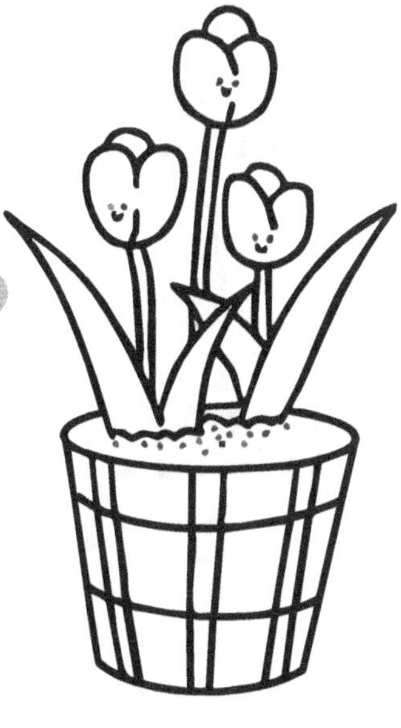

Practice for drawing here.

95.

Seeds

1.

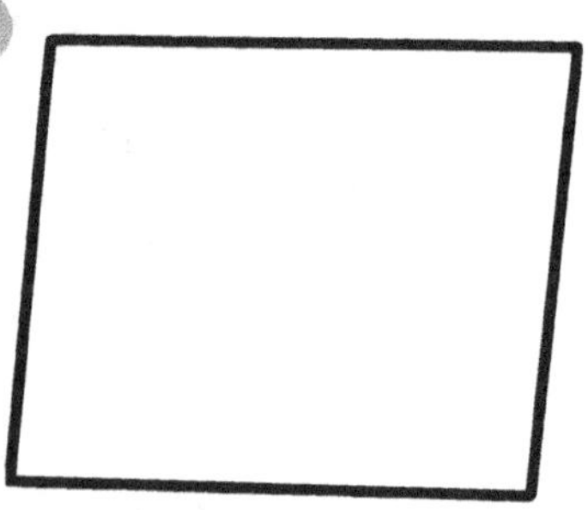

2.

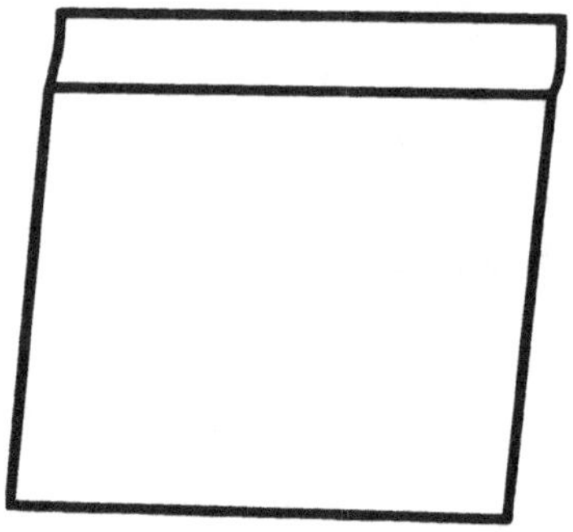

3.

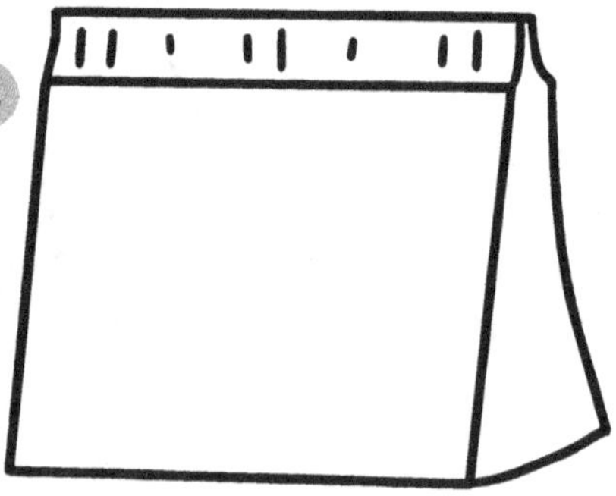

4.

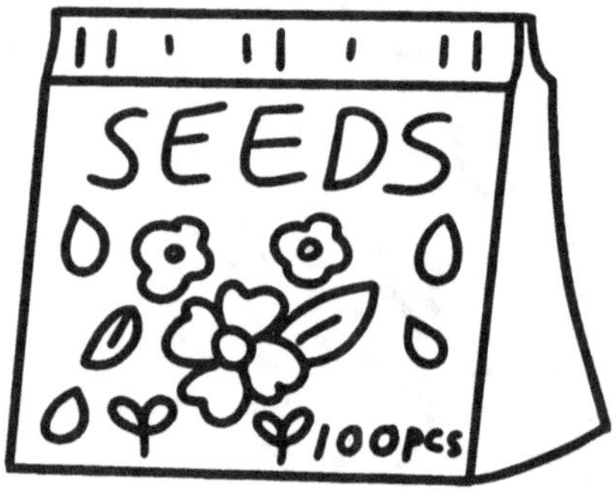

Practice for drawing here.

Snowman

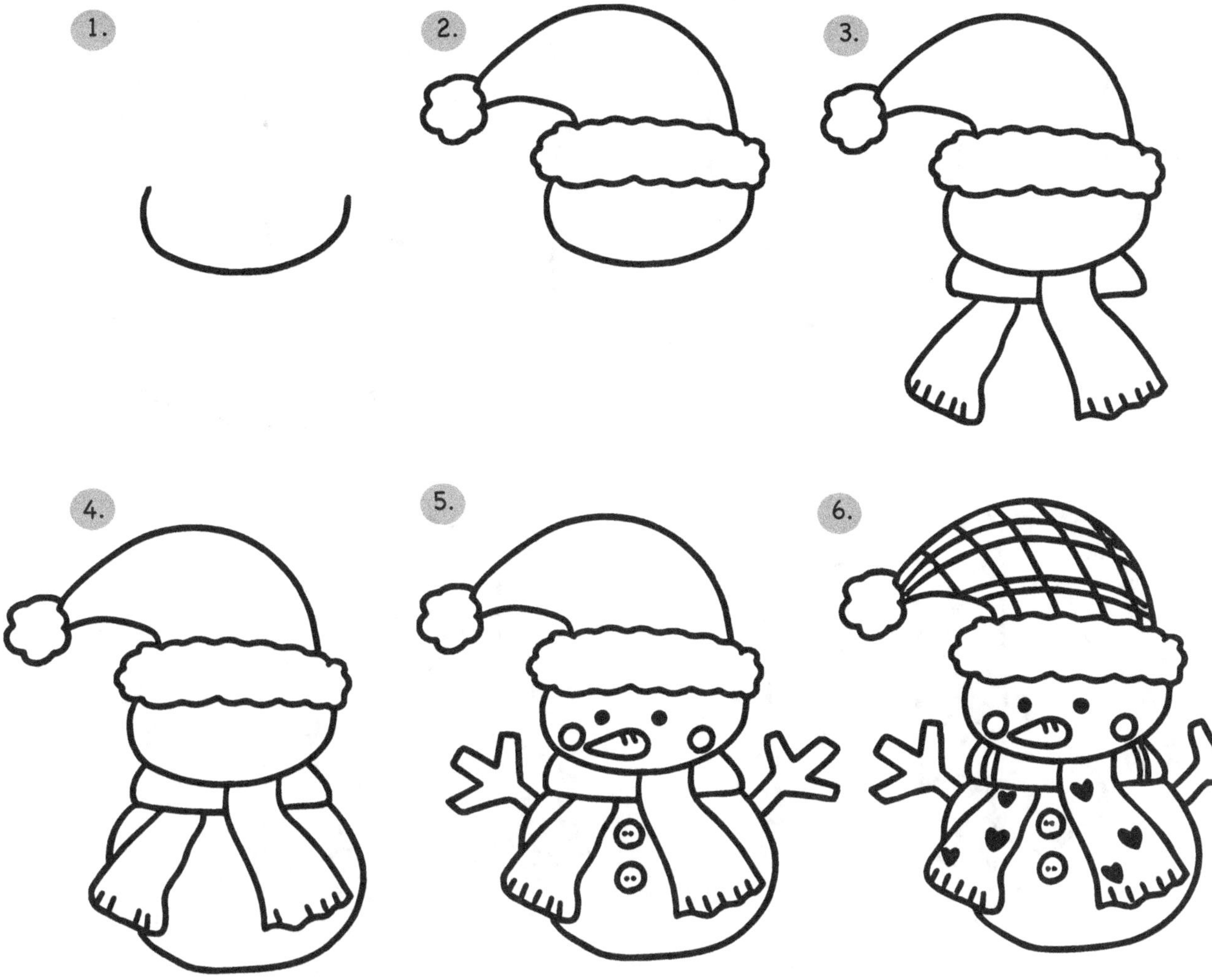

1.

2.

3.

4.

5.

6.

Practice for drawing here.

Boots

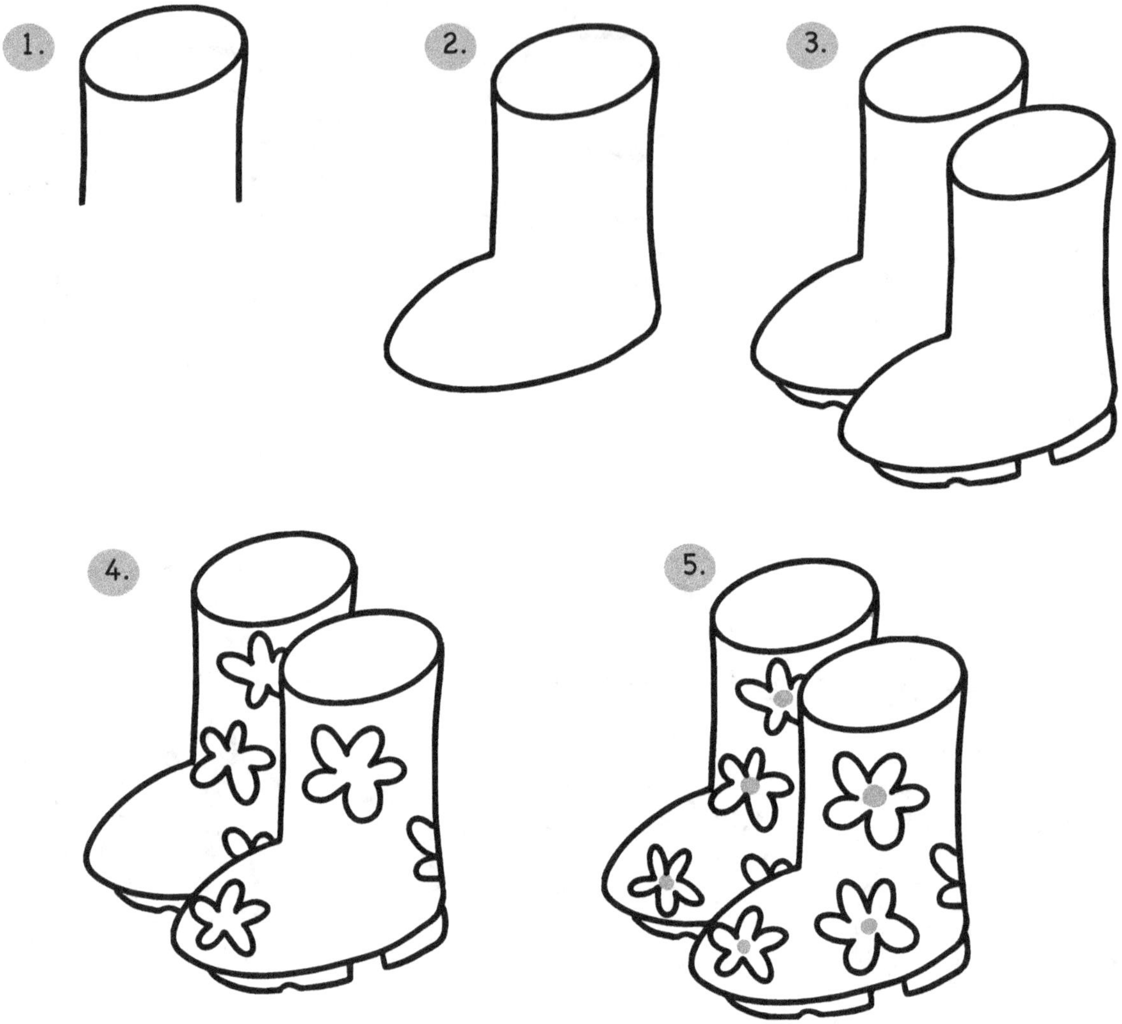

1.

2.

3.

4.

5.

Practice for drawing here.

Gardening gloves

1.

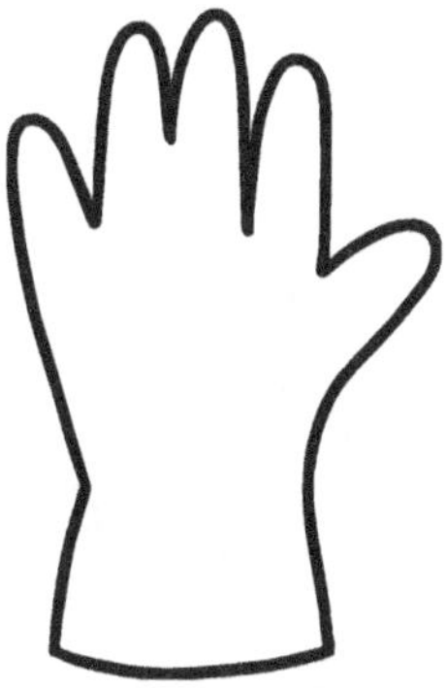

2.

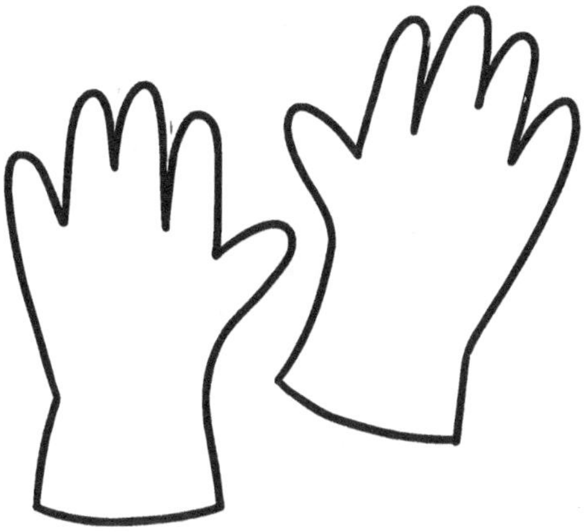

3.

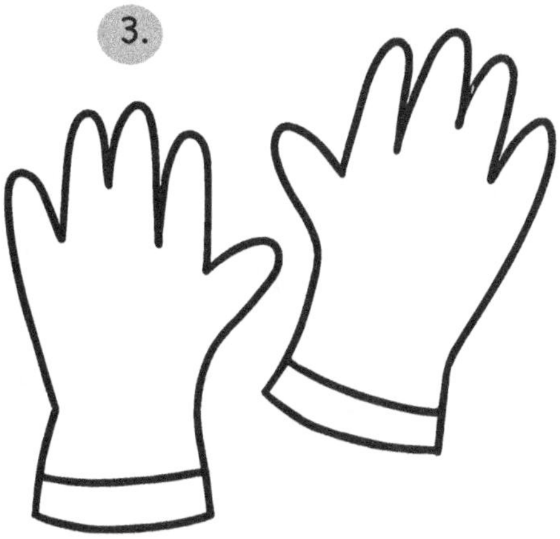

4.

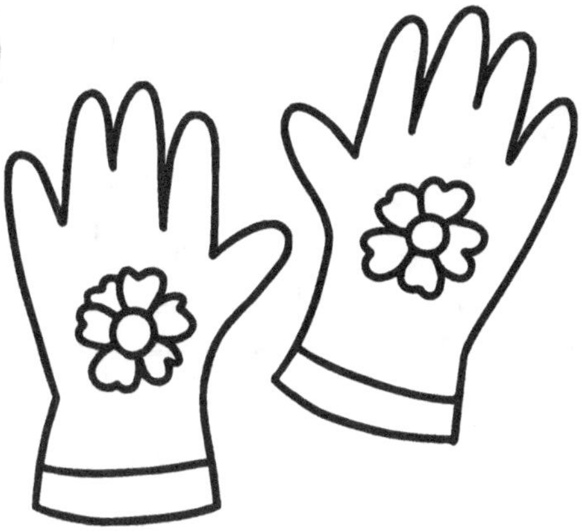

5.

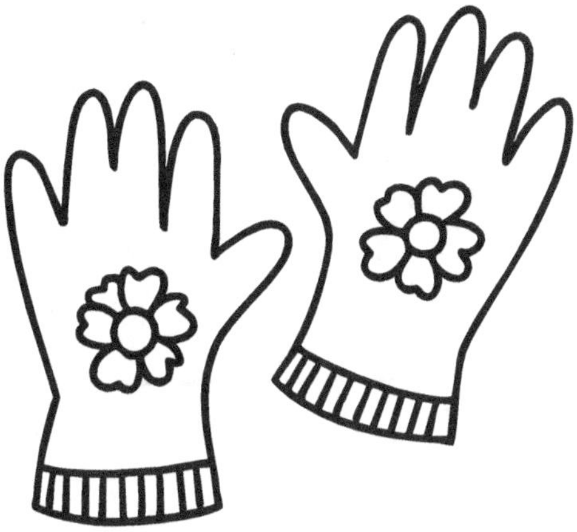

Practice for drawing here.

Watering can

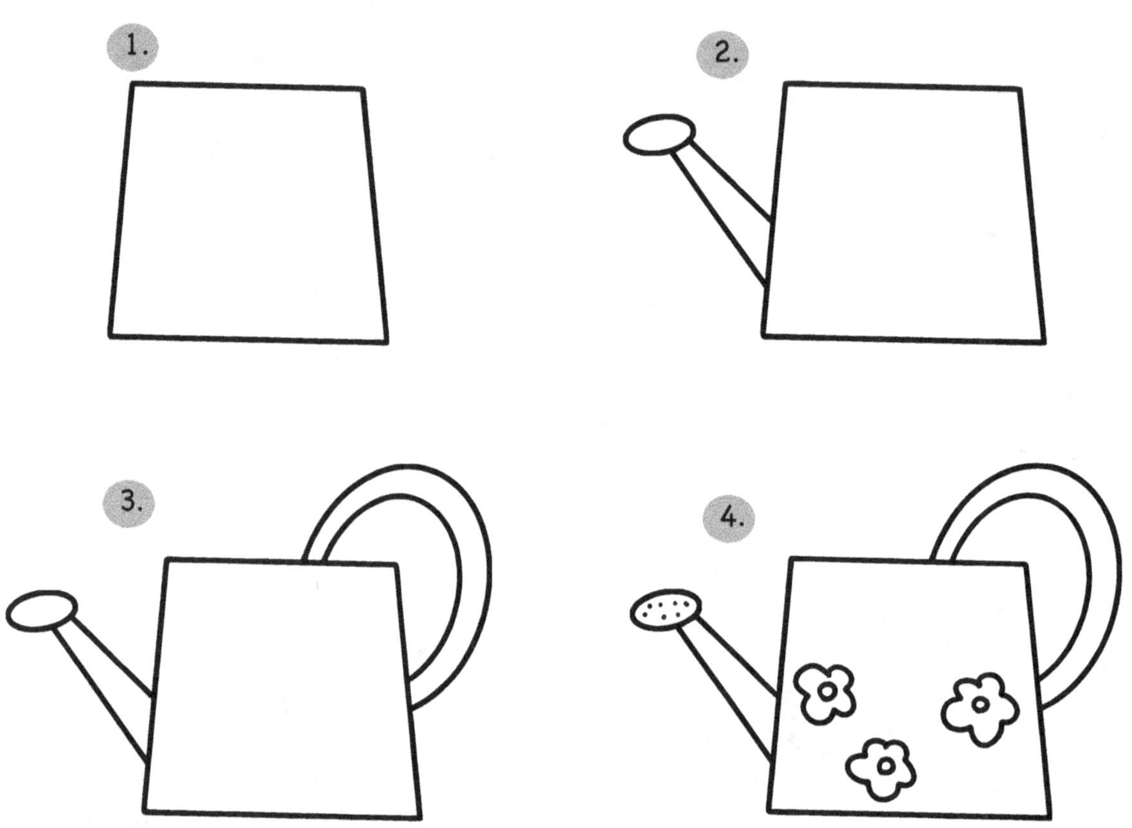

Practice for drawing here.

Woven bag

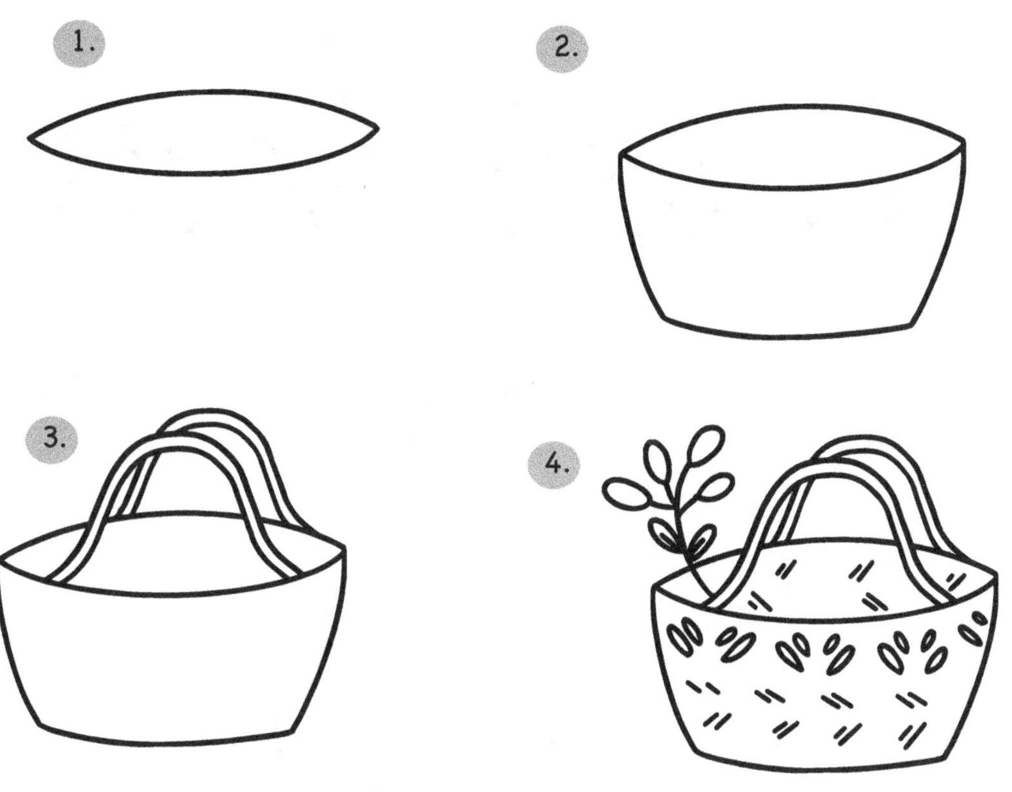

1. 2. 3. 4.

Practice for drawing here.

Thank You

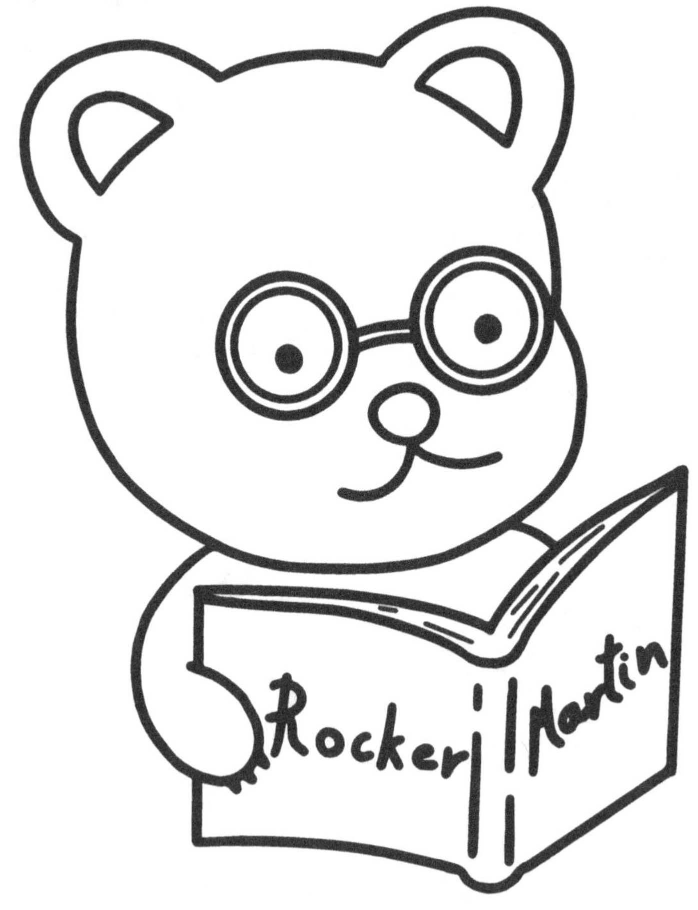